Perimeters of Social Repair

Proceedings of the Fourteenth Annual
Symposium of the Eugenics Society
London 1978

Edited by

W. H. G. ARMYTAGE
Division of Education,
The University, Sheffield

JOHN PEEL
Teesside Polytechnic,
Middlesbrough, Cleveland

1978

Academic Press
London · New York · San Francisco
A Subsidiary of Harcourt Brace Jovanovich, Publishers

ACADEMIC PRESS INC. (LONDON) LTD.
24/28 Oval Road
London NW1

United States Edition published by
ACADEMIC PRESS INC.
111 Fifth Avenue
New York, New York 10003

Library of Congress Catalog Card Number: 78–52101
0–12–062750–7

Printed in Great Britain by
Fletcher & Son Ltd, Norwich

Contributors

K. G.-A. BARLOW, *The Health Centre, 49 King Street, Thorne, Nr. Doncaster DN8 5AU, England*

A. R. BOON, *Department of Human Genetics, The University, Newcastle upon Tyne NE2 4AA, England*

MARY E. BRENNAN, *West Midlands Regional Health Authority, 146 Hagley Road, Birmingham B16 9PA, England*

P. E. BROWN, *Department of Community Medicine, University of Sheffield Medical School, Beech Hill Road, Sheffield S10 2RX, England*

KEN FOGELMAN, *National Children's Bureau, 8 Wakley Street, London EC1V 7QE, England*

VERA HOUGHTON, *Becks Cottage, Bletchingley, Surrey RH1 4QS, England*

IAN MCCOLL, *Department of Surgery, Guy's Hospital, London SE1 9RT, England*

PAMELA K. POPPLETON, *Division of Education, University of Sheffield, Sheffield S10 2TN, England*

MALCOLM POTTS, *Population Services International, Marie Stopes House, 108 Whitfield Street, London W1P 6BE, England*

MARGARET B. SUTHERLAND, *School of Education, University of Leeds, Leeds LS2 9JT, England*

SHELAGH TYRRELL, *Kensington and Chelsea and Westminster Area Health Authority (Teaching), 14 Bishop's Bridge Road, London W2 6AF, England*

W. WILLIAMSON, *Department of Sociology and Social Administration, University of Durham, New Elvet, Durham DH1 3JT, England*

Preface

This volume records the proceedings of the fourteenth annual Symposium of the Eugenics Society. Its "quality of life" theme and its interdisciplinary approach reflect the major preoccupations of the Society with biosocial issues.

The Council of the Society is grateful to all those distinguished contributors to this Symposium and the editors gratefully acknowledge the help of Miss Eileen Walters in the detailed organisation of the event and of its published proceedings.

On behalf of the Eugenics Society

W. H. G. ARMYTAGE
JOHN PEEL

Contents

Models of Social Repair: Myths and Dilemmas

PAMELA K. POPPLETON

Division of Education, University of Sheffield,
Sheffield, England

The arguments around which my paper will be structured are:

1. That the kinds of decisions we make about social problems are not pragmatic. They reflect the models that we have about the nature of society and social breakdown in particular.
2. That the *professionals* who initiate and implement decision making define the *perimeters* of social intervention. They also help to define and project the models currently in vogue.
3. That 'repair' is an antiquated concept arising from over-stress on biological analogies and medical models.
4. That other models are available. In the evolution of interventionist strategies, yesterday's models generate today's myths.
5. That alternatives presently available have environmental and political implications. They do not release us from dilemmas but pose new ones, the solution of which will preoccupy us over the next decade.

People have always sought to understand social processes by drawing analogies between social and other systems. The analogy between society and biological organisms had its strongest expression in the Social Darwinism of the late nineteenth and early twentieth centuries emphasising the principle of evolution as universal law. One of its exponents, Stanley Hall (1904) explained the problems of adolescence by referring to a theory of recapitulation in which "the individual in a general way repeats the history of its species, passing slowly from the protozoan to the metazoan stage . . ." In case we are inclined to dismiss this as fantasy it is worth recalling that the Boy Scout movement was based upon the recapitulatory model (Reaney, 1964). Scouting was thought to provide a means of satisfying various barbarian instincts such as gathering, fishing and hunting which were considered to be influential in the life of the child at that age. And scouting is still with us.

Analogies with machines proved too reductionist in nature to survive, but analogies with control systems are incorporated into the systems model upon which much organisational theory is based (Ackoff, 1974) and, with the emergence of an ecological model (Quinn, 1964) we have come back full circle to an analogy with biological processes, but this time they are those of harmony, balance and symbiosis.

How do these models relate to the 'perimeters of social repair'? In this paper, I shall take the 'perimeter' to be defined by the professionals who in their work are concerned with maintaining the well-being of individuals and groups, i.e. those who can be dimly perceived standing 'amid the encircling gloom' of good intentions which often seem to define the perimeter for those who are the recipients. It is they who make or carry out decisions which involve social interventions of one kind or another. The term 'profession' is normally applied to an occupation which has developed a systematic body of theory and culture (Greenwood, 1957) and which 'serves as a base in terms of which the professional rationalises his operation in concrete situations'. Another way of saying this is that the scaffolding of the 'repair' professions is, in effect, the model currently in vogue with which the professional supports his work. And there are alternative prescriptions which affect not only the work but the kind of thinking which the professional contributes to public discussion and which usually ends up in government reports, two of which I shall discuss.

But, first, a brief diversion on the concept of 'social repair' itself. It is a term which to many, may have a curiously antiquated ring implying some sort of structural breakdown within society and attempts to paper over the cracks. The early eugenicists would have had no truck with such half-hearted measures. They conceived of 'repair' as putting right genetic errors so as to bring about the solution of social problems arising from lack of population control (Ludmerer, 1972). It is a deeply conservative concept which appears to make no reference to changing circumstances nor to the development of new structures and may be loosely translated as ameliorative social reform. An example would be the attempts of educationalists during the 1960s culminating in the Plowden Report (Central Advisory Council for Education, 1967) to define deprivation and disadvantage and to establish the idea of compensatory education. Bernstein (1970) criticised such efforts on the grounds that

> The concept 'compensatory education' implies that something is lacking in the family and so in the child. As a result, the children are unable to benefit from schools. It follows then that the school has to 'compensate' for something which is missing in the family and the children are regarded as deficit systems.

In this sense, social repair is intervention which does not disturb the *status quo* of the education system and the nature of the intervention is related to the way in which the 'damage' is conceptualised.

An alternative interpretation of 'repair' would be one which focused on the *processes* of intervention and would imply some inadequacy in the services provided, i.e. on the nature of the schools themselves, the content and quality of the teaching and on the distribution of resources. These alternatives are particularly important for those professionals who function as change-agents in their institutions and are concerned with assessing the possibility of change. Intervening to identify weaknesses in either fabric or process and to prevent breakdown from occurring implies the need for prediction and control; both are terms which have become dirty words in the prevailing ideologies of social action. This is one of the dilemmas with which we are faced. Because the notion of intervention which carries overtones of prediction and control has become pejorative, the professional who seeks to justify the role must go in one of four directions:

(i) to a preoccupation with pathology (in which case he will be castigated for lack of interest in the broader social problems of the community).

(ii) towards an environmentalist solution, which seeks to initiate change *within* the institutional framework in conjunction with fellow professionals.

(iii) to emphasising the expressive rather than the instrumental aspects of the role by giving priority to the caring and compassionate elements. This (Halmos, 1974) is one way in which an institution can advertise its compassionate (or would-be compassionate) character without being interventionist; or,

(iv) towards involvement in the community, either by making professional knowledge and skills available to others or by deliberately stimulating community action to enable those who suffer breakdown and its consequences to bring about institutional change.

The chosen course of action will reflect the model of the social process which the professional holds and his response to the models held by others. Thus, the sense in which I use the term model is not as an all-embracing explanatory system, but rather as a *set of strategies* or method of working. The models which encompass the various strategies described can crudely be classified as the medical, the systems and the ecological models, though these are not all-inclusive nor do they reflect the many variations on this theme which exist in the literature.

Models and Myths

A preoccupation with pathology follows readily where biological analogies are drawn. The organism consists of an interrelated set of systems of bodily functioning and the individual is judged to be healthy insofar as these systems function adequately. His responses are compared with supposedly typical reactions and a deviation from these norms leads him to be described as 'ill'. Similarly for a society to be judged 'healthy' individuals and groups are categorised in terms of their departure from the norms. This defines the medical model.

The process of categorisation uses terms like diagnosis, prognosis, symptoms, disease and treatment (Bannister, 1977) making possible scientific research of a kind that has brought about great advances in standards of health. But it has also given rise to social problems. Illich (1976) has used the term iatrogenic illness to draw attention to diseases which originate from the physician. The dependent relationship between patient and doctor makes the former happy to accept that he is bronchitic, rheumatic or dyslexic; the anxiety of living with a label being less than living with uncertainty. The act of labelling may convert a medical problem into a social one. Crisis intervention may lead to hospitalisation, when the medical categorisation turns into a set of social 'facts' (Freeman and Giovannoni, 1969). A category of individuals now exists who can be described as hospitalised or institutionalised leading to implications of stigma and loss of personal rights (e.g. voting rights, loss of driving licence, etc.). Conversely, it may convert a social problem into a medical one. The restless, mischievous child who is a nuisance may be described by teachers as 'hyperactive' thus making likely the administration of tranquillisers. But the most central feature of the medical model is that it locates the problem in the individual or in those aspects of the environment that can be described in pathological terms; the family or the deprived neighbourhood.

It is the wholesale application of this model in the fields of mental health which is of great concern to psychologists at the present time. Here, as in the realm of physical disorders, a practitioner has the power to pronounce a person ill or healthy using analogies which supposedly derive from a continuum of normality – abnormality. Yet the definition of abnormality changes over time and between cultures; attitudes towards homosexuality being possibly the most vivid example. Szasz (1962) expresses the point clearly:

> ... when one speaks of mental illness, the norm from which deviation is measured is a *psychosocial* and *ethical* standard. Yet the remedy is sought in terms of *medical* measures.

The consequences of applying the medical model to social problems have been vividly illustrated by many writers in recent years. In the 1960s the study of deviance turned to examining the implications of the labelling process particularly for those who are labelled the 'social audience' (Erikson, 1962). Echoing Szasz, Erikson claimed that "Deviance is not a property *inherent in* certain forms of behaviour; it is a property *conferred upon* these forms by the audiences which directly or indirectly witness them". But the matter does not stop there; it is not only the *forms* of behaviour that are labelled, but those who evidence them and who come to be known as maladjusted, retarded, psychopathic, educationally subnormal, deprived, disadvantaged, disabled and delinquent. At the heart of labelling theory is the implication of stigma and its consequences. The hospitalised person becomes passive, accepting the role to which he has been allocated; the delinquent reacts to his social isolation by seeking solidarity with others who are similarly labelled so that his life and identity come to be organised around the facts of deviance (Lemert, 1967). Thus the deviant is seen to be as much the product of society as the rebel against it.

In the machinery of social intervention, the professional working in the public and social services often sees himself as occupying an analogous role to the medical practitioner. One attractive means of escape from the dilemmas of personal power and control is the simple environmentalist solution of identifying and rectifying those features of the environment which seem causally to be related to the deviance, i.e. positive discrimination which has been such a feature of major recommendation in recent government reports. This (Titmuss, 1968) is a device for intervening more directly at strategic points in the social structure which is "free from stigmatisation insofar as it aims at raising standards to the best possible level rather than the minimum level tolerable". But is it naïve to suppose that positive discrimination can ever fulfil these claims? First, it is still rooted in pathology, the victims of circumstances being regarded as passive and powerless; they are neither. Second, all too often the programmes are based on myths generated by the value systems within which the models are developed.

Two of the myths which are generated by the medical model are related to deficit theories which have come under attack in recent years. They are the myth of the deprived child (Ginsburg, 1972) and the myth of early experience (Clarke and Clarke, 1976). Both were accepted by the Plowden Report.

The facts of deficit are not in question, the issue is about the universality of its effects not only upon health and standards of living but upon intellectual development. Cognitive deficit is assessed to arise from the lack of a stimulating environment such as well-endowed parents can provide but Ginsburg concludes that there is almost no research evidence to show that poor children's environments are deprived in this respect, "Therefore, education need not concentrate on removing these non-existent deficiencies". It should concentrate instead on examining the deficiencies inherent in the system itself.

The myth of early experience rests on the view that the first few years of life *necessarily* have crucial effects upon later development and adult characteristics which may be irreversible. In attacking this view, Clarke and Clarke state:

> It is possible that when more deprived children are followed up through adolescence and adult life, it will be found that in many, the *critical psychological damage* . . . (will tend) to be repaired to varying extents.

These ideas will undoubtedly receive more attention from other contributions to this Symposium; suffice it to say that the implications of these myths (Bronfenbrenner, 1976) would be the professionalisation of child rearing and increasing state intervention in child-rearing practices on a scale which would imply a totalitarian state. It is a paradox that in their attempt to avoid the iniquities of the medical model, the labelling theorists fall into the same traps. It is supposed that those who are labelled passively accept the expectations of the labellers and so produce a self-fulfilling prophecy. Yet this is by no means supported by the many studies which have sought to replicate the work of Rosenthal and Jacobson (1968) which was carried out in an educational context. This is not to say that imputations of inferiority have no effect, but simply that people do not react passively to stigma. Thus, the label 'social priority school' has its basis in administrative convenience but arouses resentment in those pupils who are aware of its implications.

The second alternative means of escape from the dilemmas of prediction and control is for the professional to emphasise the expressive rather than the instrumental aspects of his role. The idea of 'corrective' intervention is replaced by concern for the whole person in relation to his/her social and cultural setting and life cycle. Thus, the individual is treated not as a 'case' in isolation from his/her own environment, but as a client with the possibility of self-referral. The role of the professional is to utilise social and psychological analysis to plan for constructive change and to marshal knowledge and resources within the service or the institution in order to maximise client well-being. Halmos (1974) describes the role as "change-initiating even if the micro-social change it can initiate registers on the social system only slowly and cumulatively". This is the counselling role and Halmos points out that it is one way in which the institution can advertise its compassionate (would-be compassionate) character without seeming to be interventionist. In this way, it is customary for schools to emphasise the function of pastoral care as a means of stressing their concern for the whole of the child's well-being as distinct from purely academic concerns.

It is an approach which has wide appeal, but one which also has its attendant 'myths' and dilemmas. One of the myths which Halmos discusses is the myth of 'non-intervention'. He says of counsellors:

> No matter how strenuously non-directive they describe their work in their protestations, their purpose is clearly to effect change through some sort of guidance. The other labels such as 'psychotherapist' or 'social caseworker' conceal this central fact of the counsellor's role.

For the professionals, the dilemma is a real one, for they must search for a rationale 'for their professional status as experts and as possessors of a credentialled skill'. To deal in the common currency of everyday life and to employ the personality to bring about change is a weak stance from which to compete with other professionals; one which drives many towards behaviourism and others to political solutions. Halmos vividly sketches these dilemmas.

Such an approach overcomes some of the more undesirable features of the medical model though, in fact, the professional must often adopt the process of categorisation to provide help, if only for administrative convenience. It does, however, include the possibility that the institution itself may be the client insofar as it is the focus of change, though in general the pressures against change are often strong enough to leave the *status quo* intact.

The consequence of accepting the myths which arise from the medical model and its bastard variations are that many of the services which deal in the mechanics of social repair appear themselves to be at the point of breakdown. Of the 14 per cent of children in ordinary schools who are estimated to have symptoms of emotional disturbance, only 2 per cent are able to have specialist help (Jones, 1975). One hundred thousand children are currently in care in England and Wales yet (Roberts *et al.*, 1977) there are enormous regional variations according to who makes the decisions. At the same time paradoxically, receipt of Family Incomes Supplement, free milk, optical and dental treatment and free prescriptions all show a massive decline over the years 1973–76. Midwinter (1977) attributes this decline to the stigma attached to the services, the complexity of their processes, the offhand-edness of officers and so on. The perimeters of community care he says, show compassion to be unperceived, resented and rejected; a situation in which the earnestness of its professional practitioners is in sharp contrast to their failure to transmit the message.

In summary, the features of the medical model as a method of working are:

(a) categorisation in order to get services. This is the way in which the system legitimises its operations and one of the ways in which administrative convenience cuts across its aims.

(b) abstraction of the people from the environment in which their problems occur or treatment of the environment as pathological.

(c) acceptance of the client as a passive participant.

(d) acceptance of the institutional *status quo*.

(e) proliferation of professionals who come to specialise in areas which are relatively isolated from each other.

They raise dilemmas which lie at the heart of the provision of public and social services today and these are questions of professional autonomy and public accountability. They are often represented in public debate as questions concerning the redrawing of professional boundaries and the professional lay relationship. I propose to examine them within the framework of two government reports; one published recently and one not yet published at the time of writing but about which there have been considerable 'leaks'. They are, respectively, the Court Report on the Child Health Services (1976) and the Taylor Report on School Managers and Governors (1977). The choice is not entirely arbitrary for one whose primary concerns are to do with education and psychology.

Two Government Reports

The Court Report refers explicitly (5.3) to "... barriers within the professions and between professions and between professionals and parents, which must be broken down so that a new quality of understanding, respect and cooperation is achieved." It is in many ways, an admirable report in reviewing present needs and the changes that have occurred in public health provision over the last 200 years. How does it tackle our two issues?

First of all, it is unashamedly interventionist. In advocating the practice of preventive medicine in its widest sense, a child health service ". . . has a responsibility to consider how it can influence the behaviour of families and children" (p. 18). Future improvement must concentrate on changing life-styles to produce a healthy society so that for example (p. 12) child battering would happen only in rare pathological cases.

Second, however, it recognises the barriers arising from the mystique of professionalism and insists that ". . . services for the very young child must not be allowed to become over professional; instead they (the professionals) must seek to work through the family encouraging its strengths and helping in its shortcomings" (p. 23).

Third, while recognising children's rights it envisages that ". . . at any time a professional who feels concern about a child's well being can require a medical examination, if necessary, without parental consent." The safeguard here would lie in better training for professionals and cooperation between them.

Fourth, such training would be facilitated by a redrawing of professional boundaries particularly within the psychological professions which would bring together common elements in the training of clinical and educational psychologists. A new discipline of child psychology is advocated (15.18) which would de-emphasise that element which includes experience as teachers in the schools but highlight the particular skills involved in helping other professionals. Psychologists would operate chiefly on an inter-disciplinary basis in district handicap teams working alongside doctors, nurses, teachers and social workers under a consultant community paediatrician, though their advisory role in schools should be increased (15.19).

Fifth, on the professional–lay relationship, the issue is "how professionalism should be delivered to and, on occasion, shared with, the layman" (p. 23). This will be resolved at national level (p. 21) by a small, powerful group of both lay and professionals ". . . a council of wise people who would meet from time to time to think about the needs of children and how far they were being met." Continuing government support for voluntary bodies is envisaged and, at district level, the Community Health Councils should continue to press for excellence in local services. But "Because we recognise that it is neither possible nor desirable that the consumer representation should be sufficient to maintain standards of service for children we are asking that the

Department of Health and Social Security assumes responsibilities for monitoring those of our recommendations that are 'implemented' by government." On the other hand (p. 25) "The laity are no longer the abject poor but the political nation who by their decisions and taxes create and sustain the services they require." Social provision should wherever possible enhance the capacities of the adult to cope with his responsibilities and make the client the agent of his own improved health. There must be an acceptance "... that the welfare services of this country must now bring into partnership the better educated and more concerned society that a hundred years of social amelioration has created" and this is to be done by harnessing the energies and interests of parents and other involved adults as the only way of meeting the ever growing demand for manpower.

There are admittedly selected passages from a lengthy Report to which one cannot hope to do justice in the confines of this paper. They are presented in some juxtaposition to highlight the ambiguities of opinion which the issues arouse. It is not meant to imply that because the Court Committee was composed primarily of those drawn from medical and para-medical professions, the reasoning and recommenda- tions *necessarily* reflect the medical model. Indeed, in many respects it strives to avoid the worst features of stigma, passivity and an over- professionalised approach. However, while stressing the importance of environmental influences, it locates these in the pathology of the family and the means by which skills are to be transmitted to the parents is left problematic. In dealing with the problems of handicap (which include learning difficulties) the child is to be abstracted from the school for purposes of assessment and treatment by those whose experience of the school environment is minimal. Educational psychologists are already concerned not only about the professional implication of direct inter- vention in schools without consultation (Trethowan Report, 1977) of a kind which formerly brought the profession into disrepute, but about the implication of treatment which emphasises adjustment to what may be adverse circumstances. While professional boundaries are attacked, the Report leaves undisturbed the question of institutional change in schools and finally, the whole operation is to be master-minded by wise people who meet occasionally. These strategies of intervention have not been helpful to education in the past and the Report's ambivalence in many areas seems to reflect what Strauss and others (1964) have called the uncertain coexistence of social Darwinism, social welfare and positivism. To others it may simply reflect an attempt at enlightened professionalism in a traditional context.

Is the Taylor Report likely to do better? Confronted with what appears to be a different set of problems; the issues to be explored also involve questions of professional autonomy and public accountability this time within the education system. Parents, pupils and teachers have been concerned about the inaccessibility of information on the ways in which school policies are formulated and the central issue for the Taylor Committee is the democratisation of school government. Apart from suspicions about political leverage, the functions of governors and managers have often seemed to exclude questions about the conduct and curriculum of schools and to leave untouched the power of professionals, particularly that of the headteacher. Schools are typical of many organisations in appearing to be unresponsive to consumer expectations and the solution which seems likely to be adopted in this case is increased representation of consumers on the Boards, i.e. *the cooptative principle*; an attempt to give the consumers a greater say in defining goals and evaluating a school's progress towards achieving them.

How effective is this likely to be? It will certainly alter consumer perceptions of unresponsiveness but it may do little more in real terms. Much will depend on the way in which representatives are elected and constituencies are defined. Another problem is the deeply conservative nature of consumer response expressed in another context by Younghusband (1970) who asked, "what happens if local community groups are opposed to the enlightened policies which social workers think desirable?" Similar questions are likely to arise about the ways in which schools have attempted to widen their roles with regard to child development and care as against 'corrective intervention'. The autonomy of the professional is nowhere held more dear than by the teaching profession and there will undoubtedly be a great deal of discussion as to where the boundaries should be drawn in areas of concern to both parents and teachers.

Nevertheless, the concerns of the Taylor Report move a step nearer than the Court Report towards implementing the fuller participation which accountability requires. It is easy to criticise the principle of cooptation on the grounds that ideas emanating from the lay public about the changes they desire are vague, inconsistent and poorly formed. The issue of accountability requires the professional to go further and assume responsibility for producing informed public opinion. It is a step which

> . . . calls for the prior professional obligation to be the systematic informing and stewardship of the laity, so that it might more independently and fruitfully engage in that professional-lay dialogue. (Midwinter, 1977)

Alternative Models

For others, this is not enough. Many now suggest that such issues can only be resolved by placing intervention in its political context (Marris and Rein, 1972; Lees, 1972). It may be political in two senses: (*a*) that it aims to decrease the sense of powerlessness felt by those who are at the receiving end of the system, and (*b*) that it aims at influencing and changing organisations, not just individuals, and therefore implies the possession of the knowledge and skills to do this either through new forms of management or through legislation. This strand of development is nowhere more pronounced than in the development of community psychology (Bender, 1976).

Unmentioned by the Court Report, radical changes have taken place in some areas of the country in the practice of both clinical and educational psychology. Critchley (1976), for example, estimated that whereas in 1969 educational psychologists in Liverpool spent 75 per cent of their time in the clinic, by 1973 over the same period they were spending 75 per cent of their time in the community. Community psychology as described by Bender includes

> . . . the desire to make psychology available and useful to a wide range of the population, not just certain narrow groups of deviants, and that such services should be near the populations they serve, and non-medically oriented.

The central feature is the concept of 'client advocacy' which is defined as 'serving the interests of the client/consumer, rather than those of the profession and its employees'. The professional now aims to demystify his calling by transmitting skills to those who have traditionally been excluded from them, i.e. parents and co-professionals such as nurses and teachers. He becomes a consultant, regarding the institution as the client as much as the individual and seeks to coordinate the range of services provided. However, whereas this has already been successfully accomplished *within* various kinds of residential provision, it is labour intensive and extremely costly. Bender points out that it does nothing for areas where services are almost non-existent and where community-based services seem to be the only way of meeting needs. It would be erroneous to assume that these are necessarily cheaper. Under Parkinson's Law, problems expand to occupy the number of helpers available and it is no accident that the increased load on the social services has followed the expansion of personnel. There will always be a grey zone between chronic need and crisis intervention in which this law operates.

The detailed strategies which such a mode of functioning implies are beyond the scope of this paper but, if we return to our framework, it is an approach which can most usefully be encompassed by an ecological model. This requires (Bronfenbrenner, 1976) "major changes in the institutions of society and the invention of new institutional forms", or even a para-institutional approach. It has much in common with the systems approach in that the central issue is one of resource management but when resources are conceptualised as including the professional himself (his time and expertise) and the mobilisation of resources indigenous in the population, then the central emphasis is on the community.

But who or what comprises the 'community'? For those who call themselves community workers it is defined (Reiff, 1966) as those of low income who live in a world of limited or no opportunities and who see themselves as victims of circumstances. The myth of community as an all-embracing concept is vividly illustrated by the recent report on *Gentrification in Islington* (Barnsbury People Forum, 1977) which deals with the problem of middle-class immigrants in working-class neighbourhoods. And the corresponding dilemma?

> . . . This is not to say that professional people cannot be useful in community affairs. They can, but unless they make their expertise available in a way that is acceptable to working-class people, they are bound to be misunderstood and resented.

It is a fair point. Client advocacy and accountability are now incorporated into the perimeters to define the limits of the intervention process. It is also a reminder that eco-systems seek to adapt to change by minimising disturbance—and the professional is a disturbing agent. Eggleston (1977) notes in particular

> . . . the ways in which all the participants in the educational process can display a vigorous capacity to preserve their ecological environment intact. It is in pursuit of this end that much of the power in the system is applied . . .

To summarise the characteristics of the ecological model, therefore,

(a) the professional–lay relationship becomes problematic. Resources include both professionals and the lay public.

(b) intervention becomes multi-disciplinary involving psychological, sociological, organisational and political skills.

(c) the location of services is a key point.

(*d*) professional status becomes problematic. The professional is engaged in an attempt to resolve the tension between self-consciousness and helping (Bender, 1976).

Thus, the model accepts the concept of deprivation but defines it in relation to the unequal distribution of resources. The sharing of professional power and skills is seen as the only viable solution.

Conclusion

In this paper I have used two Government Reports to pose some questions: Who defines deficit, deviance and repair? The legislator, the professional or the individuals concerned? Is the individual case, client or consumer; and what comprises the community? The alternative prescriptions traced force us to reconsider our models of social intervention and the place of the professional within them. It is clear that one model does not just replace another. Although the medical model is becoming unacceptable to an increasing number of professionals the alternatives do not release them from dilemmas, particularly those to do with the unresponsiveness of institutions in a changing world.

I began by saying that decision making is not a pragmatic process but reflects the models we have about the nature of society and social breakdown. But perhaps this too is a myth? Academics can afford the luxury of agonising about their models but it is equally probable that the changing constellations of opinion reflect a pragmatic response to the changing structure of the population in terms of both its overall decline and age distribution—just as the early eugenicists responded to the challenge of population increase. The Court Report may reflect little more than a changing demand for paediatric services and the Taylor Report, an investment in a contracting service. It is a tempting thought but, as Eisenberg (1975) says: "... the substitution of myths no less than the exchange of truths, is a serious business."

References

Ackoff, R. L. (1974). *Redesigning the Future: A Systems Approach to Societal Problems*. New York: John Wiley.
Bannister, D. (1977). *The Medical Model—An Epidemic Ailment*. Paper read to the British Psychological Society Conference.
Barnsbury People Forum (1977). *Gentrification in Islington*. Report. London.
Bender, M. P. (1976). *Community Psychology*. Essential Psychology Series. London: Methuen.

Bernstein, B. (1970). A critique of the concept of compensatory education. In *Education for Democracy*, edited by D. Rubenstein and C. Stoneman. Harmondsworth, Middlesex: Penguin Books.

Bronfenbrenner, U. (1976). Is early intervention effective? Facts and principles of early intervention: a summary. In *Early Experience: Myth and Evidence*, edited by A. M. Clarke and A. D. B. Clarke. London: Open Books.

Central Advisory Council for Education (1967). *Children and their Primary Schools.* Plowden Report. London: HMSO.

Clarke, A. M. and Clarke, A. D. B. (1976). *Early Experience: Myth and Evidence.* London: Open Books.

Court Committee (1976). *Fit for the Future.* The Report of the Committee on Child Health Services. London: HMSO.

Critchley, D. (1976). Conversation reported. In *Community Psychology*, p. 71, edited by M. P. Bender. London: Methuen.

Eggleston, J. (1977). *The Ecology of the School.* London: Methuen.

Eisenberg, L. (1975). The ethics of intervention: activity amidst ambiguity. *Journal of Child Psychology and Psychiatry*, **16**, 101.

Erikson, K. T. (1962). Notes on the sociology of deviance. *Social Problems*, **9**, 307–314.

Freeman, H. E. and Giovannoni, J. M. (1969). Social psychology of mental health. In *Handbook of Social Psychology*, Vol. 5, edited by G. Lindzey and E. Aronson. Reading, Massachusetts: Addison-Wesley.

Ginsburg, H. (1972). *The Myth of the Deprived Child.* Englewood Cliffs, New Jersey: Prentice-Hall.

Greenwood, E. (1957). The elements of professionalisation. *Social Work, N.Y.* **2**, No. 3.

Hall, G. S. (1904). *Adolescence—Its Psychology and its Relation to Physical Anthropology, Sociology, Sex, Crime, Religion and Education.* New York: Appleton.

Halmos, P. (1974) The personal and the political. *British Journal of Guidance and Counselling*, **2**, 131–148.

Illich, I. (1976). *Medical Nemesis.* London: Calder & Boyars.

Jones, M. J. (1975). Emotionally disturbed children in ordinary schools: concepts, prevalence and management. *British Journal of Guidance and Counselling*, **3**, 146–159.

Lees, R. (1972). *Politics and Social Work.* London: Routledge & Kegan Paul.

Lemert, E. M. (1967). *Human Deviance: Social Problems and Social Control.* Englewood Cliffs, New Jersey: Prentice-Hall.

Ludmerer, K. M. (1972). *Genetics and American Society.* Baltimore: The Johns Hopkins University Press.

Marris, P. and Rein, M. (1972). *Dilemmas of Social Reform.* London: Routledge & Kegan Paul.

Midwinter, E. (1977). The professional–lay relationship: a victorian legacy. *Journal of Child Psychology and Psychiatry*, **18**, 101–113.

Quinn, J. A. (1964). Ecology. In *Dictionary of the Social Sciences*, Vol. 17, edited by J. Gould. London: Tavistock.

Reaney, M. J. (1964). The psychology of the boy scout movement. *Pedagogical Seminary*, **21**, 407–411.

Reiff, R. (1966). Mental health, manpower and institutional change. *American Psychologist*, **21**, 540–548.

Roberts, G., Reinach, E. and Lovelock, R. (1977). *Children on the Rates.* Social Services Research and Intelligence Unit, Portsmouth Polytechnic.

Rosenthal, R. and Jacobson, L. F. (1968). *Pygmalion in the Classroom.* New York: Holt, Rinehart & Winston.

Strauss, A. L., Schatzman, L., Bucher, R., Erlich, D. and Sabstein, M. (1964). *Psychiatric Ideologies and Institutions*. New York: Free Press.

Szasz, T. S. (1962). *The Myth of Mental Illness*. London: Secker & Warburg.

Taylor Report (1977). *A New Partnership for our Schools*. London: HMSO.

Titmuss, R. (1968). *Commitment to Welfare*. London: Allen & Unwin.

Trethowan Report (1977). *The Role of Psychologists in the Health Services*. London: HMSO.

Younghusband, E. (1970). Social work and social values. *Social Work Today*, **1**, No. 6.

The Changing Role of Charities

VERA HOUGHTON
Bletchingley, Surrey, England

Not all that is charitable in the public eye is charitable in law, and much of what is charitable in law has no relevance to the modern concept of need. All religious organisations have charitable status but not all voluntary organisations. Although they may be charitable in intent, some voluntary organisations are denied the financial advantages of a charity in law. I hope to show that not only is a definition of charitable purposes long overdue but so is a new terminology to suit the changing role of charities. The term 'charity' is too painful a reminder of the days of the old Poor Law, of almshouses and ragged school-children. As such, it has no place alongside the new State-provision terminology, of supplementary benefits, guaranteed income levels and sheltered housing.

Defining Charity

The decision on whether particular objects are charitable in law is at present left to the Charity Commissioners and to the courts which are the final arbiters. This is because there has never been a precise definition of the meaning of charity. The only guide-lines are in the preamble to the 1601 Statute of Charitable Uses, long since repealed, and in case law of which there are many hundreds of cases.

Charity as seen through medieval eyes covered the relief, support or maintenance of the aged, impotent and poor; sick and maimed soldiers and mariners; schools, universities and scholars; bridges, ports, havens, causeways, churches, sea banks and highways; orphans; houses for correction; marriages of poor maids; young tradesmen, handicraftsmen and persons decayed; relief or redemption of prisoners or captives, and the easement of poor inhabitants in the payment of certain fines and taxes.

In 1891 Lord Mcnaghten attempted to classify these medieval categories under four main heads: trusts for the relief of poverty, trusts for the advancement of education, trusts for the advancement of religion, and trusts for other purposes beneficial to the community, not falling under any of the preceding heads. It is this fourth classification, trusts for other purposes, which causes so many headaches and on which there is such a volume of case law.

The Nathan Committee (1952) recommended that there should be a new definition of charity but left untouched the existing case law. It was later found impossible in the drafting of the Charities Act of 1960 to devise any 'new' definition which would not be new in substance as well as in form. The Goodman Committee was unable to devise 'a neat encapsulated definition of charity'; instead, they recommended that the categories of charities should be re-stated in simple and modern language replacing those of the 1601 Act and extending them to include objects now considered to be within the scope of charity (*Charity Law and Voluntary Organisations*, 1976). The new recommended list is as long as the alphabet. When it comes to the education of the public generally, there is a proviso that 'no attempt is made to influence the public by propaganda'.

Permissible Education and Political Propaganda

The boundary separating education from propaganda and political activity is so thin as to be hardly discernible except to the Charity Commissioners who drew it. Uncertainty about the degree of permissibility has resulted in some organisations forgoing or forfeiting charitable status because they found that development of their work was dependent on being able to apply pressure for official provision or for a change in the law, and because they lacked the funds to take their cases to the High Court.

In their Report the Charity Commissioners (1969) admitted the "obvious difficulty in determining exactly where this boundary lies but if a charity . . . issues literature urging the government to take a particular course or organises sympathisers to apply pressure . . . to their elected representatives, we think it is clear that the boundary has been overstepped". They then go on to advise that "it is probably unobjectionable for a charity to present to a government department a reasoned memorandum advocating changes in the law provided that in doing so the charity is acting in furtherance of its purposes". But at the same time they warn that if an organisation does anything ancillary to its charitable purposes, further difficulties may arise "in defining the boundary between what is merely ancillary and what amounts to adopting a new purpose in itself".

Religious Charities

The biggest paradox in the modern role of charities is the position of religious bodies. Long before the Statute of 1601 it was regarded as self-evident that the advancement of religion was of benefit to the community and therefore charitable. For some four hundred years religious teaching directed the charitable impulses of the rich to help the poor and distressed, but always with a moral purpose. It was not enough to be poor: the poor had to be deserving and 'deserving poor' were invariably those of good character, who neither drank nor swore, who were quiet and orderly. Charity schools for the poor were not only for learning but for the encouragement of virtue which usually meant diligence and obedience.

It was not the Churches that fought to remove the social conditions and injustices which the big charitable institutions of the nineteenth century sought to remedy: Dr Barnado's Homes, Shaftesbury Homes, the National Children's Home and Orphanage, Children's Aid Society, the Salvation Army and many more, all founded to deal with the casualties of the Industrial Revolution. It was the institutions themselves that were instrumental in bringing about the big social reforms of the early twentieth century—the Old Age Pensions Act of 1908, the National Insurance Act of 1911, the Midwives Act which became operative in 1910, the Housing and Town Planning Act of 1909. In appealing for support they had to identify the social evils they were trying to overcome. As a result the emphasis changed from bandaging the wounds of society to preventing the injuries, and the charitable approach began to take on a political aspect which today threatens the charitable status of some organisations.

The difficulty that the Churches have in translating the abstract ideals of justice into practical propositions relevant to everyday life emerges in Clifford Longley's review (1977) of the British Council of Churches' latest essay *Understanding Inequality*. "The authors find plenty of evidence of poverty and deprivation in contemporary Britain and quote statistics to show that two children in every British classroom are likely to come from homes which combine bad housing and low incomes and include either four other children or only one parent." Yet church groups and organisations are shown to be inadequate and confused when asked to think seriously about political and economic matters. "The particular contribution of Christian insight into inequality is that it can be changed and does not have to be accepted as the unalterable consequences of capitalism, or the inescapable result of heredity, or the result of unresolvable consequences of class warfare." "But", says

Mr Longley, "like other essays in the same field, this one falters when it reaches the question: 'How?' and can only offer modest and local remedies."

Non-religious charities in a position to promote more radical and far-reaching remedies would, however, be constrained from doing so by the restrictions placed on political activities, restrictions which do not apply to religious bodies.

An Escape Hatch

It is interesting to examine the reasoning of the Charity Commissioners when asked to state why certain inflammatory statements made by Church leaders at the time of the February 1974 General Election were not in breach of charity law. These and other statements were submitted in evidence to the Goodman Committee in 1974 by Mrs Diane Munday who has had the experience of working with a political pressure group (the Abortion Law Reform Association) and with a registered charity (the British Pregnancy Advisory Service).

The Secretary to the Charity Commission replied as follows: "The authors of the articles or the persons whose views are being reported might reasonably claim that their views relate to issues of morality and behaviour which are quite properly of interest to religious organisations and that insofar as they are seeking to instruct, exhort and influence the behaviour of their readers they are seeking to advance religion in accordance with the tenets of their faith. If, however, it is argued that, insofar as the persons concerned are seeking to organise their sympathisers to apply pressure for changing the law of the land, they are indulging in political activities, the question then arises whether such activities affect the charitable status of the institutions concerned ... whether the activities are merely ancillary to the charitable purposes of the institution or form such a large proportion ... as to constitute in effect a new or additional purpose ...". The view is expressed that "taken in the context of the total work of the Roman Catholic Church or of the Church of England, or of the other recognised Christian denominations, these particular activities form such a small part ... that they fall far short of being political activities ... if indeed they are political activities at all" (Charity Commission, 1974).

Challenged on the suggestion that they are not political activities at all the Charity Commission took refuge in the observation that "The pursuance of political activities relating to issues of morality and behaviour by religious charities would not in the normal way be objectionable because such issues are an essential concern of religious bodies and therefore it is not likely to be outside the powers of any charity having wide religious objects to engage in such activities" (Charity Commission, 1975).

It is this sort of metaphysical reasoning that brings down calumny on the heads of the Charity Commissioners ("a fine selection of vituperative epithets have been levelled at them" in the evidence to the Goodman Committee) and makes a convincing case for a legal definition of charitable purposes.

New Religions and Ethical Bodies

The present system becomes even more anomalous with the acceptance of fringe or freak religions as charities. Mr Ben Whitaker, in his Minority Report to Goodman, asks "What law court or human agency empowered to demarcate charitable status is competent to judge the validity of a religion or the genuineness of a new guru (if applicants must produce a satisfactory miracle, then Mr Uri Geller might appear a strong claimant) or claimant to be a new Messiah?"

With the recognition of these new religions there can be no justification for continuing to rule out ethical bodies such as the Humanist Trust and the National Secular Society. The Goodman Committee (1976) considered that "in principle, the advancement of such movements should be brought within the ambit of charity" subject to certain provisions. "Those seeking charitable status for the promotion of movements of this type whether religious or not should be required to satisfy the Charity Commissioners or the court that their advancement is for the benefit of the community according to certain basic concepts . . .". For instance, "a political party should not be permitted to masquerade under the cloak of an ethical or philosophical system", and society "has a duty to determine what is and what is not beneficial to it; accordingly between good and evil it cannot be neutral".

Research Bodies

A further example of the vagaries of the present system is the tendency of the Charity Commissioners and the courts to regard research and dissemination of its results as not being a charitable activity "if it is directed to furthering a particular point of view or if it tends to establish a climate of opinion or to inculcate an attitude of mind". The Goodman Committee thought this was going too far and referred back to the publication of Darwin's *Origin of Species*. Despite the considerable controversy this publication aroused at the time, the Committee had no doubt that "the research which went into that work and its dissemination was an activity which could properly come within the ambit of charity". Be that as it may, if history repeated itself today there would be a strong likelihood that opponents of Darwin's theories would be organised to challenge the research body's charitable status, such threats now being part of the armoury of organisations of opposing views.

Allegations and Accusations

Next to propaganda and political activity, the most damaging charge that can be made against a charity is that it is engaged in a commercial venture. While the ultimate aim is to persuade the Charity Commissioners to remove the offender or victim from the register, there are some useful side benefits. The amount of unfavourable press publicity suffered by the victim and the time and effort that have to be expended in refuting the allegations, not to mention the cost of taking legal advice, all add to the value of harassment. Pregnancy advisory charities are particularly vulnerable. The identity of the organisation (if there is one) behind the complaint may not be apparent though the victim usually has a shrewd idea; if an individual the complainant may be a doctor in private practice.

In 1976 the pregnancy advisory charities (British Pregnancy Advisory Service and Pregnancy Advisory Service) were accused of being in league with the pro-abortionist lobby and of promoting abortion on request. It was alleged that a very high percentage of the pregnant women who consult these charities go on to have abortions. But the Charity Commissioners took the view that "it is no more than natural that a large proportion of the women who consult such a charity rather than their family doctor are likely to want abortions if these can lawfully be given". The Charity Commissioners explained that a charity cannot arrange an abortion if this would be unlawful and that each case must be decided on the facts and on the medical advice based on those facts (Charity Commissioners, 1976).

The Family Planning Association also came under fire in 1976. The chairman and vice-chairman (Mrs Jill Knight, MP, and Viscount Ingleby) of the Parliamentary all-party Family and Child Protection Group, sent an Open Letter to the Charity Commissioners expressing the view that the FPA should no longer qualify for charitable status and asking the Commissioners to consider whether the Association should remain on the register. This self-appointed Parliamentary Group argued their case under four main headings: that the FPA is a commercial venture; that it has a political object; that it has assisted in and connived at breaking the law, and that its purpose is the mere increase of knowledge. The Charity Commissioners invited the FPA to comment in detail. Other organisations and individuals on both sides joined in the correspondence. The Charity Commissioners published their findings in the 1976 Report. Having made a careful investigation the Charity Commissioners could find no grounds for further action on their part and decided that the FPA should remain on the register.

'Privileged' Comment

Another method of undermining charities whose work is controversial is to attack them in Parliamentary debates, knowing that there can be no immediate rebuttal and that the allegations will go unchallenged in Hansard, the Official Report, for all time. This happened to the FPA in January 1976 in a House of Lords debate on Sex Education, when the Association was attacked by a number of Peers of whom the leading spokesman was Baroness Elles. The FPA had no option but to issue a lengthy statement refuting the many incorrect and misleading allegations made in the debate, but by the time it was released it was no longer newsworthy (Family Planning Association, 1976).

During the Second Reading debate on Mr William Benyon's Abortion (Amendment) Bill in February 1977, Mrs Elaine Kellett-Bowman, MP, attacked the pregnancy advisory charities, accusing them of paying vast sums in salaries to their directors, administrators and surgeons who, she alleged, put up the money in the first place. "It is total hypocrisy to pretend that there is anything remotely charitable in the normally accepted sense of the word in the way they behave. Their counselling is normally confined to suggestions to their victims as to how to raise the cash to pay them."

Mrs Kellett-Bowman's attack was answered three months later in a paper "The truth about the charities" delivered by Diane Munday (1977). Mrs Munday compares their salaries with those of other charities, including the anti-abortion charity Lifeline of which Mrs Jill Knight, MP, is chairman. At the end of her paper Mrs Munday speculates about the reasons for these unprincipled and inaccurate attacks. "It is my contention . . . that it is the existence of bodies like BPAS and PAS that has forced down the price of abortion in the private sector . . . and has forced up the standards of care and concern offered to women . . . While high fees were being charged for commercial abortion, while women were being exploited by taxi-touts and

others, while scandals hit the headlines, the anti-abortion lobby could
. . . win support for their declared aim of reducing abuse and exploitation." Now that abuse and exploitation have practically disappeared,
in large part due to the very activities of the charities under attack, Mrs
Munday suggests that the anti-abortionists are having to resort to lies.

Clarifying and Extending the Boundary of Political Activity

The Goodman Committee found a general lack of knowledge and
understanding of the present law, many charities being under the impression that all political activity was prohibited. They recommended
that greater political activity should be permitted to charities subject to
the following guide-lines:

(*a*) that political activity should not be an object of the charity nor a
     principal activity such that its charitable object is in effect
     displaced by the extent of its political activity;
(*b*) that political activity should be and be seen to be ancillary to the
     object of the charity;
(*c*) that political activity should not include direct or indirect financial
     or other support for or opposition to any political party or
     individual or group seeking elective office, or any organisation
     having a political object.

Where there is "duality of function" and the political activity of an
organisation is outside the guidelines, the Committee "would prefer to see
greater separation rather than unification under a charitable banner".
They saw nothing objectionable in the same group of people promoting a
body with charitable objects and another body with political objects. Mr
Whitaker, however, thought that "it should not be public policy to put a
premium on hypocrisy".

Any idea that these guide-lines might possibly apply to religious
bodies was dispelled earlier in the Report by an unequivocal statement
in evidence from the Churches that "involvement in the realms of
politics must be regarded as an essential manifestation of church life at
times and nothing must be done which might hinder the Churches
from organising deputations and doing what they can to influence
public opinion". This means that priests can continue to denounce
Parliamentary candidates from the pulpit with impunity.

The major criticism that these recommendations still leave the
decision in the hands of the Charity Commissioners and the courts was
recently expressed by Lord Ponsonby of Shulbrede, chairman of the
Charity Law Reform Committee, an independent body composed of

members drawn from a wide variety of voluntary organisations. In a debate on the Goodman Report in the House of Lords on 4 July 1977, Lord Ponsonby criticised the Goodman Committee for tackling the central problem of charity in such a way that "if the proposals are enacted, vagueness and uncertainty of law will be increased". A mass of new case law would be created; "not case law created in the courts but case law made by the decisions of the Charity Commissioners at individual points of time, as to what is or what is not a charity".

Non-profit Distributing Organisations (NPDO)

Because of the impossibility of small organisations challenging the decisions of the Charity Commissioners in the courts, the Charity Law Reform Committee has recommended a new form of charitable organisation known as the 'Non-profit distributing organisation' (NPDO) which would enjoy the financial advantages at present accorded only to charities. The Goodman Committee dismissed this proposal as being tantamount to abolishing altogether the concept of charity as it has developed over the centuries and as altering radically the commonly accepted meaning of charities in the minds of most people. Indeed, Lord Goodman, in the House of Lords debate, described it as "the most bizarre suggestion we received". Lord Ponsonby saw no alternative if the evident need for fairness, clarity and certainty was to be met.

Charities Board

To assist the Charity Commissioners the Goodman Committee proposed the creation of an independent Charities Board with a chairman and members independent of the Charity Commission, who would include those with experience of the new activities in which charities are involved as well as the traditional activities.

The functions of the Charities Board would include advising the Charity Commissioners on matters of policy and administration including provisional registration of charities, removal of charities from the register, conduct of inquiries, review of charities, conduct of surveys and collection of statistical data. Public relations and investigation of complaints against the Charity Commissioners would also be within the purview of the Board as well as the appointment of local committees and the conduct of local reviews. The Home Secretary would be responsible for the appointment of the chairman but the members of the Board would be appointed by such bodies as may be specified in the new legislation.

The Value of being a Charity

Relief from taxes of one sort or another goes back to Elizabethan times and with the imposition of more and bigger taxes over the centuries it has now reached a staggering figure. This so-called 'fiscal benefit' of charitable status is important not only to the larger 'big-business' charities, like Oxfam and the Spastics Society, but equally to smaller local charities, particularly in the case of covenanted donations and relief from rates.

Charities are almost completely exempt from income tax and corporation tax; they are entitled as of right to 50 per cent relief from rates, and local authorities may, if they wish, give additional relief. Charities do not pay capital gains tax on disposals by them. They enjoy certain advantages under the Community Land Act, 1975, and under the Development Land Tax Act, 1976, and they benefit from limited reliefs on VAT and stamp duty.

Relief from income tax or corporation tax is estimated to amount to some £75m per annum, including sums amounting to £20m to £22m recovered under covenants by charities. No estimates are available of the value of the other reliefs.

Among further concessions proposed are an increase in mandatory relief on rates from 50 per cent to 75 per cent to be borne centrally; relief from the general service charge; a reduction in the period for covenants from seven to four years, and tax to be recoverable at the higher rate subject to an upper limit (at present only standard rate tax can be recovered). The Goodman Committee also recommended that the comparatively new development of forming charity companies for trading purposes "should not be interfered with".

No relief of any sort is proposed for voluntary organisations not having charitable status though they may be providing an equally valuable and non-profit making service to the community. Rather than extend the definition of charity to include NPDOs, the Goodman Committee would prefer that the government give separate financial aid, where considered appropriate, in the form of grants, subsidies, loans and reliefs.

It is questionable whether the continuance of all these tax reliefs to charities even at present levels can be justified especially when other voluntary organisations are left out in the cold. Mr Whitaker believed that a system of priorities should be established and that "the first priority should be to concentrate these primarily on deprivation and the disadvantaged . . . to include . . . lack of human rights and education".

The principle of giving tax reliefs to charities is so entrenched and the 'interested parties' so numerous that any attempt to discriminate between one charity and another, to cut reliefs or to abolish them altogether would probably be met by a greater outcry than if it were proposed to give tax exemption to all NPDOs.

The Goodman Committee were satisfied that if a balance were drawn, the advantages to the community derived from charitable funds and services would far outweigh the cost of the taxes and rates forgone. If the immense amount of unpaid effort put into charitable work by trustees and voluntary workers could be costed, it would add up to an enormous sum.

Adjusting to Change

The continuing contribution that charities and associated voluntary organisations can make to community life lies in their flexibility, in their ability to pioneer and to experiment. They can be ahead of public opinion and can initiate programmes which governments would be too nervous to introduce without some evidence of public support. They can be pacemakers as well as pathfinders. Voluntary action has not only frequently pioneered the way for State action, but when a service has been taken over by a statutory authority, the voluntary organisa-tion has continued to provide a valuable supplementary agency.

With the refinements of social welfare provision, new types of organ-isation, charitable and non-charitable, have evolved to help people obtain their rights and to work for the removal of anomalies: charities such as Shelter, Child Poverty Action Group, Gingerbread, Age Concern, and non-charities such as the Disablement Income Group. The latest development in this field are the self-help organisations which the Goodman Committee described as "a small group of people joining together to pursue charitable objects which are of concern to them". They include organisations to help rape victims, battered wives and children, artificial-kidney users and back-pain sufferers. Their founders provide enthusiasm and sometimes expertise in a particular subject but few or no funds: having no endowment they depend wholly on appeals to the public and to grant-making charities and agencies.

Charity Overseas

The relief of poverty, distress and suffering abroad is no less deserving of help than at home. The Goodman Committee recommended that no distinction should be drawn and that any object charitable at home should also be considered in principle charitable when carried out abroad, provided that it was not "contrary to the public policy of the United Kingdom or of the country where the activity is undertaken". An example of charitable activity contrary to the public policy of a recipient country is, of course, proselytising missionary work which some countries have banned on becoming independent. Where foreign missions have been allowed to remain, their work is now confined to education of a non-religious nature and medical aid. To safeguard the public interest of the UK the Goodman Committee recommended that "there should be a procedure whereby the Foreign Office can make an order requiring the charity to stop that activity".

The Charity Commissioners expressed a more restrictive view in their Report (1963) in relation to overseas work fulfilling the Mcnaghten fourth criteria of other purposes beneficial to the UK community. They pointed out that "public works or development projects such as roads and irrigation . . . will generally be charitable only if they are a reasonably direct means to the end of relieving existing poverty in observable cases; but they appear not to be charitable if the purpose is the general economic improvement of another country". Benefit to the United Kingdom community, however, might arise from charitable purposes for the general benefit of a British Commonwealth country which is in close association with the UK. The Goodman Report reproduces the relevant extract *International Activity* in an appendix.

There are doubts too about the extent to which charities operating overseas may be indulging in political action when, for example, helping victims of internal warfare or in pressing for more government aid to developing countries. Mr Whitaker suggested that "if, instead of financing projects abroad, Oxfam concentrated on education, propaganda and political pressure in Britain which resulted in the government increasing its present net aid budget by even 10 per cent, vastly more 'poverty, distress and suffering' would be relieved overseas".

The school activities of such charities as Oxfam, War on Want, and Population Concern, the fund-raising body in the UK for the International Planned Parenthood Federation, are helping to build a new generation of donors which is attracted by the idea of voluntary service overseas, of working alongside the youth of other countries, and of trying when they return home to narrow the gap between the developed and developing countries.

Moving into the Future

The old association of charity and moral reform has gone. Today, social justice, helping the deprived and disadvantaged, human rights and political consciousness are the new charitable impulses. The growth of State provision and bureaucracy, however sensitive and understanding, takes something away from the democratic involvement of members of the community in matters of common interest and concern. Charities should therefore be widening their horizons rather than narrowing them, in order to compensate for the growing power of central government, and to enlarge the degree of participation. The so-called participation in parliamentary and political processes is too remote for most people: they look for something more accessible, more practical and more positive. Voluntary or community service offers this. A simple definition of charitable purpose might then be any purpose beneficial to the community, and the two fundamental conditions for qualification the purely voluntary nature of management and full accountability of income and expenditure.

References

Charity Commission (1974). A letter. 29 November.

Charity Commission (1975). A letter. 12 February.

Charity Commissioners for England and Wales (1963, 1969 and 1976). *Reports*. London: HMSO.

Charity Law Reform Committee (1974). *Charity Law—Only a New Start Will Do*. Leaflet. London: The Charity Law Reform Committee.

Charity Law Reform Committee (1975). *A Public Privilege—Not a Private Right*. Leaflet. London: The Charity Law Reform Committee.

Family Planning Association (1976). *FPA Statement on the Sex Education Debate in the House of Lords*, April. London: Family Planning Association.

Goodman Committee Report (1976). *Charity Law and Voluntary Organisations*. London: Bedford Square Press.

House of Lords (1976). Motion on 'Sex Education of Children'. *Hansard*, **367**, No. 18. London: HMSO.

House of Lords (1977). Debate on 'Charity Law and Voluntary Organisations'. *Hansard*, **385**, No. 85. London: HMSO.

Longley, Clifford (1977). 'Seeking a Christian answer to poverty and deprivation'. *The Times*, 26 September. London.

Munday, Diane (1974). A letter. 4 November.

Munday, Diane (1977). The truth about the charities. In *Abortion: the NHS and the Charities*. A Symposium. London: Birth Control Trust.

Nathan Committee Report (1952) on the Law and Practice relating to Charitable Trusts. London: HMSO, Cmd. 8710.

Budgeting for the Repair Bills

MALCOLM POTTS
*Director, Population Services International,
Marie Stopes House, London, England*

Some of the biggest problems in administration go unresolved as a result of their sheer size. The most cost effective allotment of the resources available for health care is one such problem.

Resources

To see problems in perspective we must start outside the health system. In 1974 England spent £4000 million or 5·59 per cent of the Gross National Product (GNP) on its health services. By contrast Canada, with half the population, spent nearly twice as much, or 6·5 per cent of her GNP. Most developing countries spend less than 2 per cent of their GNPs on health and social services. The target for the Philippine government, the Philippines being a relatively wealthy Asian country, is to spend 0·7 per cent GNP on health by 1980. Seventeen out of sixty-five poor countries devote less than $1 per capita per year to health against $520 for Canada.

Before we can divide a budget we need to decide how large it should be. The fundamental question "what percentage of the gross national product does the nation wish or it is prepared to spend on health?" is not decided in any open, rational way, yet the budget for social repair cannot be infinitely elastic. It will probably never exceed 10 per cent of any country's resources, but in most situations people will wish it to exceed 1 per cent. In the short term, the budget for health care is not going to double or even grow by 5 per cent in a single year, nor is it likely to be significantly reduced in absolute terms. We need better ways for society to discuss and then explicitly set the percentage of the GNP to be devoted to health and social repair.

Allocating Resources

However inadequately the total budget is decided, the need for a rational allocation of available resources is obvious. During the 1960s the National Health Service (NHS) budget grew at about 4 per cent per annum while population grew by 0·2 per cent. Now the budget is stationary and the problem of setting priorities, which could be avoided previously, must be faced. "No overall growth in public expenditure is planned beyond the level now envisaged for 1976/1977" (Department of Health and Social Security, 1976a).

PRESENT SYSTEMS

The White Paper (Ministry of Health, 1944) setting up the National Health Service sketched a state response to a perceived demand for health care, without either appreciating that the demand might be open ended or foreseeing the need to set priorities. The goal was simple:

> To ensure that everyone in the country—irrespective of means, age, sex or occupation—shall have equal opportunity to benefit from the best and most up-to-date medical and allied services available.

It was to be achieved by allowing "people to choose their own medical advisors" and "freedom for the doctor to pursue his professional methods in his own individual way and not be subject to outside clinical interference". No consideration was given to selecting priorities.

Today, the recognition of the need to set priorities by administrators occasionally generates almost poetic bureaucratic language—

> the purpose of planning is to ensure that major decisions, including resource allocations, are made by statutory authorities in advance in the light of available facts and after examining alternative courses . . . the process would consist of an annual planning cycle updating the rolling ten-year plan—a four-year plan based on notified financial target—and a less detailed projection for a further six years. (Department of Health and Social Security, 1972).

The Civil Service tries to follow trends, such as the current one for decreasing the length of hospital stay, as well as being sensitive to political pressures. The Department of Health and Social Security (DHSS) creates a consultative document (*Priorities for Health and Personal Social Services in England*) (Department of Health and Social Security, 1976a) laying out some of the options that exist, emphasising priorities which have been developed by doctors or within the political system and this, in turn, produces a feedback from professional bodies,

Area Health Authorities and others. The Minister then attempts to digest the whole of this material before final decisions over priorities are taken.

But other forces are also at work. There is what might be termed *setting priorities by scandal*. The campaign by the *Sunday Times* (1972–73) on behalf of thalidomide damaged children highlighted a health need. If the media calls attention to, say, poor conditions in mental hospitals, then more resources get switched to that field. Sometimes, events of public health significance force themselves upon the public, even though neither the medical profession nor the media initially recognise the need for change. The great London smog of December 1952 did not draw immediate comment from the medical journals, and newspapers headlined the destruction of some prize animals at the Smithfield Agricultural Show long before they highlighted the ninefold increase in bronchitis deaths, associated with the prolonged fog. Yet ultimately, it was this single dramatic event which led to the clean air legislation that, for a small investment, has brought great public health benefits (Hall *et al.*, 1975).

Incidentally, a 10 per cent reduction in bronchitis was estimated to save the NHS about £3·7 million a year in the 1960s (Office of Health Economics, 1962).

As a generalisation, one may say that the public, politicians and the media are more likely to respond to immediate causes, such as bronchitis deaths during a week of fog than they are to long-term relationships, such as cancer of the lung, heart disease and the other maladies associated with prolonged smoking.

In the British democratic system, pressure groups are able to exert leverage on public decision making. The Child Poverty Action Group and Shelter are contemporary examples, while the Family Endowment Society (founded in 1918) is a classic historical example of a pressure group which began a twenty-year struggle for family allowances.

SETTING PRIORITIES

The role of the medical profession itself in setting priorities is anything but straightforward. Goals are often sorted out in what might be called the *medical market place*. Cases can always be made out for special needs—the aged, the handicapped, kidney transplants, research or whatever. Unfortunately, the leverage of human suffering acts unequally in the effort of doctors to extract resources. It is easy to retreat behind slogans such as "the highest standards" or more cleverly "not letting standards fall"—slogans which justify a share of the available resources by emotional blackmail, rather than by looking at the reality of the total available budget.

The sidestepping of issues which began in the 1944 White Paper continues in the 1976 DHSS Consultative Document:

> There is no question of interfering in clinical decisions, but a realistic review of service priorities must involve discussions with the profession on the extent which resources can be released.

The DHSS calls for the "use of low cost solutions wherever this can be done without damage to standards of care", but, in management terms, the subclause can easily negate the prior statement. You cannot have your administrative cake and eat it. Ultimately, somebody has to say that economic limitations must affect clinical judgement.

Medicine is less scientific than is commonly thought. For example, the incidence of tonsillectomy is probably best regarded as a fashion, rather like the height of a woman's hemline, rather than a response to medical need. (If tonsillectomies were reduced by three-quarters, it would save £4·5 million a year.)

Society itself imposes restraints on the deployment of resources. The general practitioner, the health visitor and others most close to the community are often best placed to make judgements about the additional resources which may be required to keep the elderly, mentally handicapped or other sick people in the community and out of institutional care. The greater the freedom to use resources, the more efficient that use is likely to be. However, the greater the delegation, the more likely it would be that a minority of personnel would embezzle or misuse funds. Whenever such cases occur they receive the full glare of media publicity "the tax-payer/rate-payer's money is being wasted!" Therefore, we take away freedom of action from personnel and hedge it about with rules, committees and supervisory staff who supervise the supervisors, even though this may use more money than any misuse of money that might occur.

Therefore, at present, priorities evolve slowly and imperfectly: new needs must find a vehicle of expression and fight for legitimacy, the feasibility of new ideas must be discussed and, finally, a perceived need gains a wide basis of democratic support and begins to be translated into possible action.

MEASURING SUCCESS

No adequate system has been devised for measuring health and social welfare needs. A former Minister of Health said "real needs must be identified". Many people see such earnest pleas as searching for the end of the rainbow. There is on consensus on issues as broad as whether the individual should express his perceived health needs, or whether the doctor should assess them. The hypochondriac who sits in the doctor's surgery or the undiagnosed diabetic who sits at home are obvious examples of basic problems in defining health needs. At the present moment, the DHSS largely relies on intermediate variables through the Hospital In-Patient Enquiry, the General Practitioner Morbidity Survey and other such measures. Unfortunately, these measures side-step crucial administrative questions concerning whether cases should be admitted to hospital at all, or the division of resources between keeping the aged in the community or keeping them in residential homes.

Doll (1976) has written of the need to monitor health services according to the outcome of treatment, the social acceptability of the services that are offered and their economic efficiency. He emphasises that the total mortality rate (at least up to the age of 65 years) is the most sure marker of health service effectiveness, as well as being a good indicator of morbidity trends.

Donaldson (1976) has shown very effectively how micro-epidemiological studies can be useful in identifying needs. In his comparison of the most deprived urban areas of Teesside with the rest of the community, he identified about one-fifth of the population as having multiple problems, from high levels of atmospheric pollution, poverty, unemployment, the absorption of recent immigrants to a mortality ratio which was nearly 55 per cent higher than that for the rest of the community.

Several commonly used measures of health care revolve around hospital beds. The physical structure, medical staffing, administrative procedures and public image of a hospital are all oriented towards a patient who is in his pyjamas. Doctors can be obsessed with beds. They are emotionally significant in the relationship between the doctor and the patient. One of the ways a doctor asserts his superiority is to take off the patient's clothes.

Beds are an economic counter. The size of a hospital is measured by its number. Consultants have a number of beds which is a symbol of their status and often a direct measure of the resources available to them. Yet remarkably few conditions in medicine require you to remain immobile, horizontal and deprived of the dignity of clothes. A great many people in hospital today are having investigations which could have been conducted in an out-patient department, are there for "bedrest" which could have been carried out at home by a flexible and less costly use of health service resources. Finally, some people are in hospital beds for no other reason than that the beds exist.

The phrase has been coined that "nature abhors an empty bed". For example, bed occupancy in Guy's Hospital stayed constant in the ten years from 1951 to 1961, although the population of the surrounding area decreased by more than 10 per cent. It is inferred that doctors consciously or unconsciously admit less seriously ill patients to keep their beds filled (Acheson *et al.*, 1961).

To summarise so far: currently the health budget is still treated as an open-ended cheque. To give limits to the budget could make it easier to set priorities. In Britain, health is part of the Department of Health and Social Security. In the USA the comparable department is one of Health, Education and Welfare. The long-term aim should be to divide all the resources which society devotes to health, social welfare and education rationally, cost effectively and with social and geographical justice. A pound spent in health, in reality, is a pound less for education.

A Hierarchy of Health Care

Britain is neither a fully planned economy, nor does it permit the more painful aspects of *laissez-faire* competition. Likewise in medicine we should remember that while many of the resources are centralised and come out of taxes, some still come direct from the citizen's pocket to meet his perceived personal needs. Illness, like most things, begins in the home and the decision whether to go outside the domestic economy in solving health problems is so universal and significant that it is easy to miss it out of the total picture of health care.

For simplicity, I am omitting any mention of care by private physicians. Like private education, it is important for some individuals, it can be argued that it relieves some strain on public services, but it rarely alters decisions about those services *per se*. It is a highly political issue on which we may all have private opinions, but it is not relevant to my main arguments.

Britain has three main levels of health care. There is do-it-yourself home medicine which largely relies on the over-the-counter trade in non-prescription drugs as its therapy. Second, there is general practice and its growing team of associated professional workers, such as health visitors and community nurses. Lastly, there is institution care, either for treatment in an acute hospital or for long-stay patients, such as the aged or mentally handicapped people.

The perceived *need* for health care is an inverted pyramid (illustrated in Fig. 1(a)) with a large number of people who feel vaguely unwell and a small number who actually end up in hospital. Approximately 75 men and 85 women per thousand of a population report restricted activity due to ill health in a sample period of two weeks (Office of Population Census and Surveys, 1975) and, in 1954, the Horders (Horder and Horder, 1954) found that over a three-month interval,

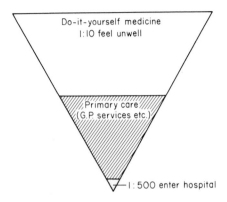

(a) The pyramid of health need in any two weeks

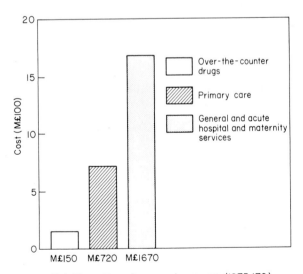

(b) The pattern of expense in one year (1975/76)

during which a sample of patients made 190 first visits to their general practitioner, they actually complained of 544 items of illness. Over the course of a year, approximately two-thirds of the patients on a general practitioner's list may visit the doctor, less than 1 in 7 will be referred to hospital and most of the referrals will be for out-patient care (Logan, 1954). Wadsworth *et al.* (1971), in a survey in Bermondsey, found 95 per cent of those questioned had experienced some symptom of ill health in the previous two weeks, although only 20 per cent had seen their general practitioner. However, the *cost* of health care is broad-based with very expensive hospital services, moderately expensive general practitioner care and a totally self-sufficient over-the-counter line of home treatment (Fig. 1(b)). Indeed, the State lifts some money in profit, taxes and VAT from do-it-yourself medicine.

HOME MEDICINE

The innumerable private decisions that we all make about whether to treat ourselves or seek outside help are an unresearched area, but the available data suggests most of us make reasonable choices. Certainly, no country from the Peoples' Republic of China to the USA has ever bypassed self-medication. The choices individual people make in such matters are often as valid as those of any centrally planned system to deal with minor illness. Ninety-six per cent of people questioned by Cartwright (1967) said they would see their doctors over unusual vaginal bleeding in a woman, but only 45 per cent if they had difficulty in sleeping for a week. Over-the-counter medicines are a necessary part of health care: if every person with a headache saw their general practitioner the National Health Service would stop working in one day. A study in the late sixties found 40 per cent of people had used a medicine within the last two days and half the drugs used were obtained without prescription. More than twice as many analgesics and seven times as many antacids are self-prescribed as physician-prescribed (Office of Health Economics, 1968).

The personal financial break on over-the-counter medicines may also be useful. As a member of society, I do not feel any obligation to pay for my neighbour's aspirins, although I might well feel that society should assist with the care of his wife in labour, or extend special services if he is unfortunate enough to have a mentally defective child. In 1966 the NHS spent £188 million on prescription drugs and the public £79 million on home remedies. In today's terms the latter figure must be between £150 and £200 million.

Over-the-counter medicines are abused, but probably not in any qualitatively different way to prescription medicines (Caranasos, 1974). A more creative partnership between the remedies of the street-corner pharmacist and individual health care could be attained. I suggest that society has the responsibility to ensure that over-the-counter medicines are not harmful or seriously financially exploitive. In America in 1971 $42·5 million was spent on advertising antacids which sold for $108·8 million (Graedon, 1976). But in general, it could be unwise to be obsessive about their efficaciousness or the size of profit margin of over-the-counter medicines. Placebos seem to be essential to modern living and I would prefer that people pay for them themselves than trouble their general practitioner who will only prescribe a more expensive drug, with the added danger that they might be pharmaceutically dangerous.

On the whole, the political left have attacked the trade in home remedies and dwelt on what they considered to be excessive profits, while the right has upheld the virtues of private enterprise. Both have missed a possible creative partnership between do-it-yourself medicine and the state system. I would also like to suggest a new initiative to link over-the-counter medicines and health education. Why should the innumerable non-prescription remedies for chest complaints not tell us to see our doctor if we cough up blood? Why not tell people the difference between the bleeding that comes from haemorrhoids and that which may be a symptom of cancer?

Finally, some part of the cost of family planning services can be transferred into the over-the-counter trade if the recommendation of the Joint Working Group on Oral Contraceptives (Department of Health and Social Security (1976b)) are accepted. They concluded that "nurses, midwives, health visitors and *pharmacists* have the relevant skills and knowledge which would enable them to be trained *to prescribe oral contraceptives*." (Italics added)

GENERAL PRACTICE

Primary health care consumed £718 million out of a total budget of £3992 million in 1975/76 or 18 per cent. Of this sum, the largest single portion went on pharmaceutical services which spent £432 million on the 335 million prescriptions that were written in 1975.

The cost of prescription drugs is a good example of conflict between ideals of clinical freedom and the realities of economic necessity. Tens of millions of pounds a year could be saved if it were possible to impose what are known to be scientifically valid choices concerning drug effectiveness and costs. As it is, many doctors still do not know how much

most drugs cost, respond to brand images more than to phar-
macological facts and yield to patient pressure for prescriptions as the
simplest way of clearing their surgeries. The desire for a pill to cure
every ailment is one of the reasons for the open-ended budgets associated with the health service. The single commonest expectation of a
patient approaching a general practitioner (two-thirds of cases) is that
they will receive a prescription—and this, of course, is exactly what
most patients get (Stimson and Webb, 1975). It would be fanciful to
suggest that the public could be educated to drop this perceived need,
but I think it would be realistic to suggest that more of it could be
transferred into the over-the-counter medical services which are so
consistently omitted from health planning. They receive no mention in
the DHSS Consultative Document.

Non-institutional budgets are expanding (+3·8 per cent between
1975/76 and 1979/80) more than the total health budget (+2·1 per
cent). It is anticipated that home nurses and health visitors employed
by the local health authority will expand by 6 per cent a year which
could lead to overall economies in the long run.

INSTITUTIONAL CARE

Approximately one in ten of the population will be admitted to hospital
each year. General and acute hospital services and maternity care take
£1670 of the health budget, or 41 per cent in 1975/76. This is almost
two and a half times as much as goes into primary care. The average
cost of acute cases continues to rise, even though the number of in-
patient beds and the average length of in-patient stay has declined
recently from an average of 13·4 days in acute beds in 1965 to 10·2 in
1975. Unfortunately, when reviewed at the local level, there seems no
way in which hospital staff are able to transfer resources saved on in-
patient care to those things they would like to do on a day care basis.
The market-place struggle for resources can be particularly ruthless
within an institution, although this is the very place where greater
delegation of decision making would allow a more rational deployment
of resources.

These trends are particularly marked in maternity services where
total number of births has fallen by 5 per cent a year in the early
seventies, patient stay has declined and yet the cost of services rose by 4
per cent a year.

Services for the elderly, mentally handicapped and children have a
budget of £1328 or 33 per cent of the total DHSS turnover.
Institutional budgets will grow in absolute terms but fall in relative

terms in the next decade while the resources allotted to the elderly and mentally handicapped will grow, the former from 12·5 to 15·5 per cent of total budgets and the latter from 4·4 to 5·1 per cent.

CHANGING THE BALANCE

The process which decides which individuals and when cross the frontier between do-it-yourself medicine and general practice or when the general practitioner asks for hospital admission are of the utmost importance. A few per cent increase in the hospital population would distort the total repair bill. Ten per cent less people seeing their general practitioners would greatly lessen the strain on the National Health Service.

The scope for change at both the main frontiers is considerable. One would hope that in an increasingly well-educated, consumer-oriented world that more and more self-medications would take place and that it would be linked with improved knowledge of when the individual should seek professional help. At the second interface between general practice and institutional care great savings could be made by dealing with many surgical problems as out-patient cases. For example, hernia, haemorrhoids, varicose veins, abortion and other minor gynaecology, squint and cataract operations, as well as many biochemical and X-ray investigations, can often be performed as out-patient procedures.

A different and more limited approach to a cost-effective health service, bridging the gulf between planning and individual choice, would be the type of intermediate administration which charitable organisations offer. It has been asserted that the Family Planning Association might be able to provide a level of family planning care now assumed by the NHS at approximately half the cost. A charity, as a focused response to a limited range of community needs and bringing together people of energy and goodwill, short-circuits a number of administrative problems. Charities can often deploy resources more effectively than the state system. Large organisations find it difficult to maintain high staff morale. At the same time, there are obvious limitations to charitably run services which tend to be associated with very specific problems—such as abortion, the care of patients with disseminated sclerosis, and adoption.

Prevention Before Cure

I take it as axiomatic that preventive medicine is preferable to curative medicine and I have suggested one way of extending public health messages into the world of domestic medicine. In state health services preventive medicine should receive first priority. In 1975/76 £15 million or 0·4 per cent of the total budget in England went specifically into preventive medicine.

The control of bacteria and viral infections is cost effective and already at a high level in developed countries (Department of Health and Social Security, 1976c) although outstanding problems remain in relation to the rare but inevitable iatrogenic illness attending, say, immunisation. Should the State pay for those who suffer? Our choices are to let the individual suffer, sue the doctor, or for society to set up some kind of insurance system. I would like to see education on the unavoidable risks of preventive medicine, but would suggest that society as a whole might underwrite such risks. I would also extend these arguments to the use of oral contraceptives.

Cancer and other non-infective diseases, such as heart disease, are problems in preventive medicine only beginning to receive sensible evaluation. The single most important step that could be taken would be to reduce cigarette smoking. More men have died from diseases associated with cigarette smoking since the end of World War II than died in that war. Eight times as many people die from cigarettes than in accidents and nine times as many working days are lost due to cigarette-induced morbidity as through strikes. Incidentally, although the NHS drug bill could be reduced, it is well to remember that we spend, on average, as a nation, 1·6p a day (1974 prices) on NHS medicines and 11p on smoking. Early detection of cancer can be useful, but there is nothing comparable to the preventive actions which can be taken in relation to infective disease. While continuing to look at the problem of early cancer detection, curative experience should be evaluated more closely. Radical surgical "treatments" such as for breast cancer, should not be provided simply because society feels impotent before a sad disease. Some of our current approaches may be based on false premises, just as blood letting, dry cupping or the long interval of hospital in-patient treatment after delivery have all proved to be based on fallacies when scientifically investigated.

To prevent cancer, as opposed to detecting it and attempting to care it, requires extensive epidemiological research. This is also true of congenital defects, many of which may be traced back to factors active during gestation. Record linkage and disease surveillance using modern computerised techniques are essential. Means need to be devised to ensure confidentiality in such study areas. Over the millennia the individual physician has established the credibility of his confidential handling of information at a face-to-face level. In the modern society, similar credibility needs to be established in relation to the collection of statistical data, which in the long term is going to be just as valuable to the individual as personal interviews with the doctor.

But even prevention has to yield to economics. Vaccinations against measles might cost £500,000 a year and produce an annual saving of £100,000, but screening the population for latent diabetes could cost 2·6 million more than it would save (Office of Health Economics, 1962; 1960 prices).

The compulsory wearing of seat belts would cost little money to enforce, but it is estimated would prevent 15 to 20 per cent of all serious and fatal accidents, saving the NHS £50 million a year. However, modifying tractors to make them safer might only save one life for every £100,000 spent and Akehurst (1976) has estimated analogous safety modifications in fishing trawlers could demand an investment of £1 million per life saved. The cost of altering building regulations to prevent another Ronan Point building disaster with the possibility of death, might cost £20 million per life saved—clearly, there must be an upper limit to the cost of prevention as well as the cost of curing.

The Developing World

For the bulk of the world's population the problem of budgeting for social repair is dramatically more severe than in the West. Government resources are more limited and may not even provide for the necessary range of free vaccinations. Yet the precedent of State support for health services is occurring at a relatively earlier stage in the evolution of services than it did in the West. The choices that have to be made are more stark and simple. The criteria which defines health needs, as Sai (1977) has set out, are primarily demographic, mortality statistics (with particular reference to the mortality during the first four years of life) and nutritional status (which is open to objective measurement). These easy-to-measure, largely unmet needs must take precedent over the expressed "wants" of the community for institutional service or Western-type general practice.

In the developing world key issues concern division of budgets between community services and hospitals, the division of the medical team between auxiliaries and Western-trained doctors and the division of resources between preventive and curative medicine.

The people's own ability to pay for medicine is extremely limited and even when services are free people may not have the income to be able to afford to travel to get them. In addition, people's choices are less sophisticated—many a Third World citizen may be more afraid of tuberculosis than childhood diarrhoea, although the latter is the more frequent killer.

However, the extreme nature of the problem in the developing world sometimes throws up solutions that may be useful in the developed world. What might be called the mechanisation of diagnosis and treatment, or checklists to identify at-risk groups, such as pregnant women who may require institutional care, are being pioneered in some countries such as Tanzania. They have proved easy to teach to auxiliaries and may well find a place in the West, perhaps even for the patient to use. This type of medical practice may appear faceless, but it is cost effective and sometimes more accurate than the conclusions which come from the most gentle of bedside manners.

The developing world is also understanding the defects of current medical education. Mahler, the new Director of the World Health Organisation, who is bravely attempting to put that expensive dinosaur in a new direction, has written off the need for medical schools to,

> prepare doctors to deal with rare cases which are hardly ever encountered, rather than with the common health problems of the community: for cure rather than for care. They tend to forget that technical solutions must respond to social goals, not dictate them. Medical practice has become almost synonymous with curative medicine. And doctors are trained to look predominently at episodes of disease, pay little or no heed to the whole man, and his interaction with society (Mahler, 1977).

Conclusions

The switch that occurs, as nations become more affluent, from private medicine to State assistance in health and social security, transfers decision making about priorities in medicine from individual consumers to a centralised administration. For a long while, this basic problem was not understood and is still not fully appreciated. Systems are emerging to attempt to select priorities in such a centralised administration but they are still at a relatively unsophisticated level.

I suggest that it would be prudent for society to recognise that the resources available for social repair are finite. It might consider more direct ways of dividing these resources than the vulgarities of the medical market place, or decision making in response to media scandals.

Some of the measures of perceived health needs bypass key questions and it would be useful to pay greater attention to those forces which determine what percentage of people who think themselves sick cross the interface between do-it-yourself medicine and general practitioner care and, subsequently, between general practice and institutional care. Relatively small adjustments at each of these transfer points could result in significant savings in resources.

The problems and limitations of planning hugely complicated health and social services should encourage us to ask if the sum total of individual choices, which were the basis of private medicine until relatively recently, may not still contribute to the most cost effective use of resources. We should not denigrate do-it-yourself medicine; rather we should look to ways in which it can make a more creative impact on the nation's health. We should look positively at the advantages which charitable and independent organisations can offer to certain specified aspects of health care, such as family planning.

Preventive medicine is usually more cost effective than treatment but, even here, economics set an upper limit on what is feasible. Hippocrates, or whatever group of thinkers created the oath ascribed to him, lived in a world of private practice. He did not recognise the economic forces influencing medicine because individual patients made their own choices. Today, when the State pays, economic forces must be recognised. I would suggest that doctors are ethically obliged to use available resources as cost effectively as possible and that this moral obligation is likely to become an increasingly important one in the future.

References

Acheson, R. M., Blaney, R., Butterfield, W. J. H., Chamberlain, J. and Scott-Brown, M. (1961). *The Guy's Outpatient Study*. Confidential report to the staff and governors of Guy's Hospital. Quoted by Acheson, R. M. and Hill, D. J. (1976) *In Seminars on Community Medicine*, Vol. 2. Edited by R. M. Acheson, D. J. Hall and L. Aird. London: Oxford Medical Publications.

Akehurst, R. (1976). Quoted in The price of a life. *World Medicine*, **12** (25), 5.

Caranasos, G. J. (1974). Drug induced illnesses leading to hospital admissions. *Journal of the American Medical Association*, **228**, 713–717.

Cartwright, A. (1967). *Patients and their Doctors*. London: Routledge & Kegan Paul.

Department of Health and Social Security (1972). *Management Arrangements for the Reorganised National Health Service*. London: HMSO.

Department of Health and Social Security (1976a). *Priorities for Health and Personal Social Services 1976*. London: HMSO.

Department of Health and Social Security (1976b). *Report of the Joint Working Group on Oral Contraceptives*. London: HMSO.

Department of Health and Social Security (1976c). *Prevention and Health: Everybody's Business*. London: HMSO.

Doll, R. (1976). Monitoring of government statistics. In *Seminar in Community Medicine*, Vol. 2. Edited by R. M. Acheson, D. J. Hall and L. Aird. London: Oxford Medical Publications.

Donaldson, R. J. (1976). Urban and suburban differentials. In *Equalities and Inequalities in Health*. Edited by C. O. Carter and J. Peel. London: Academic Press.

Graedon, J. (1976). *The People's Pharmacy*. New York: St. Martin's Press.

Hall, P., Land, H., Parker, R. and Webb, A. (1975). *Change, Choice and Conflict in Social Policy*. London: Heinemann.

Horder, J. and Horder, E. (1954). Illness in general practice. *The Practitioner*, **173**, 177–187.

Logan, W. P. D. (1954). Morbidity statistics from general practice. *The Practitioner*, **173**, 188–194.

Mahler, H. (1977). Tomorrow's medicine and tomorrow's doctors. *WHO Chronicle*, **31**, 60–62.

Ministry of Health (1944). *A National Health Service*. London: HMSO.

Office of Health Economics (1962). *Factors which may Effect Expenditure on Health*. London: OHE.

Office of Health Economics (1968). *Without Prescription*. London: OHE.

Office of Population Censuses and Surveys (1975). *The General Household Survey, 1972*. London: HMSO.

Sai, F. T. (1977). *Defining Family Health Needs, Standards of Care and Priorities*. Occasional Essay No. 4. London: IPPF.

Stimson, G. and Webb, B. (1975). *Going to see the Doctor*. London: Routledge & Kegan Paul.

Wadsworth, M. E. J., Blaney, R. and Butterfield, W. J. H. (1971). *Health and Sickness: The Choice of Treatment*. London: Tavistock Publications.

Medical and Social Interaction

SHELAGH TYRRELL

*Kensington and Chelsea and Westminster A.H.A. (Teaching),
London, England*

Parents of severely handicapped children are not receiving the sort of help they most need, in spite of considerable financial support, in spite of social service commitment on a large scale, in spite of personal health services and child development centres.

This is sometimes interpreted in terms of their own feelings: that having a handicapped child at all produces such great distortions that it is not surprising parents feel dissatisfied. If a careful look is made at the delivery of the service, however, rather than the services themselves, the parents' case would seem to be quite strong. The reasons for this, and possible solutions, are starting-points in the discussion on medical and social interaction.

A recent report (Bradshaw, 1977) looked at a sample of families, taken from the total of 40,000 who had applied for help from the Family Fund since its inception in 1972. The Family Fund was set up originally to help families with congenitally handicapped, and now all with severely handicapped, children. To qualify for help, the child has to be seriously affected, and in the majority of cases, the handicap is multiple. The survey showed that the number of satisfied customers was small.

FAMILY FUND

A Sample of 303 Families from 40,000:

47 per cent had received one visit only, or none, from the Health Visitor

45 per cent of families found her "no help"

75 per cent had received only crisis contact with the Social Worker

11 per cent had regular visits from the Social Worker

The health visitor called rarely, certainly less often than might be expected in a case where the child was normal. When she did call, her visits were appreciated as someone to talk to and not for any specific help she could give. In fact, a frequent comment was that she knew nothing about handicapped children. Similarly, social workers rarely visited although when they did this was considered helpful. But they were always prepared to offer 'crisis help'; as indeed, we all are. At least you feel you are doing something and the client is grateful.

The two greatest areas of failure shown in this report, were the failure to provide a central information service and the failure to provide practical help.

An information centre is needed where all kinds of questions can be answered, and where a check list can be made to ensure that the family is receiving all the help available to them. Whatever the information, whether social, educational, medical, financial; whatever the problem (how to get a baby sitter, how to fill in forms, how to get advice for the problems of the normal siblings caught up in the dilemma of the handicapped child)—a sympathetic person manning the desk and telephone would either solve problems herself, or know to whom to turn. A service like this could be situated in the Child Development Centre, and perhaps manned by staff working with the local voluntary organisations.

The second area of failure is the subject of this paper. That is, the lack of practical advice by someone who really understands the problems and has arrived at some answers. This advice could be given by a teacher working through the parents, in their own homes.

We know that parents want it and it happens in other countries, and in other parts of the United Kingdom. The 'teacher' may be a specially trained health visitor, an occupational therapist, or someone with a psychologist training, but whatever her background her object is to guide the parents so that they (the parents) become the teachers. Where there is a District Handicap Team in existence, and hopefully this very positive aspect of the Court Report will be taken up in most places, then the expertise available in the team will support the teacher in all aspects of her work.

I am not now talking about education programmes in the child's own home, recommended to start at two or three years of age, but the very early months of life, or as soon as the handicap is recognised. As a result, there may be no firm diagnosis, but this is unimportant as the child will be needing help, the parents will be willing to give it, and if the child turns out after all to be a very 'late developer', only good can come from the early stimulation.

The children we particularly want to help are those who appear not to respond to sound; who appear to be nearly blind; who have some congenital deformities of the hand and fingers; and those whom we suspect will develop slowly, such as babies with Down's Syndrome. The stages of development are important, but more important still are the goals for which to aim.

The teacher needs to work with a very full understanding of normal development, the wide variations within this, and the knowledge of how the various handicaps may distort progress. The child will continue to need assessment by the Child Development Centre, and the parents will understand, surely to their relief, that this sort of assessment is not concerned with ultimate limits, but with the present levels of functioning, how these can be strengthened and developed further (Reynell, 1976).

I suggest that we look at the progress made by a normal child in the first year of life. Within that year, he has progressed from mass total responses at birth, to independent standing and often walking, to precision movements of finger and thumb; he has an understanding of objects, and their properties; he has learned to manipulate his environment, and he has a good symbolic understanding. The word 'cup' (although he cannot say it) means the cup he drinks from, the pleasure of drinking, and probably other cups too, for by now he has some idea of a general property we might call 'cupness'. Perhaps most important of all these intellectual accomplishments, he is aware of the permanence of objects. In other words, the ball that has rolled out of his sight still exists, even if he cannot see it. And his social relationships are even more crucial, particularly with his parents, for if they were to disappear from him, his whole world would collapse.

This is the period that Piaget refers to as the sensory motor period; a coordination of action and perception that goes so fast it can scarcely be followed—more an explosion than a progress. Maria Montessori calls this the period of 'ésprit absorbant' during which learning is almost a reflex; the child can scarcely stop himself from learning.

The normal child learns through exploring, listening, seeing. His discoveries whet his curiosity to explore further. The handicapped child may be immobile, or restricted in the sensations he receives. His experiences are limited, his curiosity not aroused, and so often he turns back into himself. How can we help him when he reaches a stage on his developmental pathway where he is blocked? A lot of ingenuity may be required on his part, and on the part of his first teachers, his parents, if he is to find some other way to progress. If he cannot progress, his handicap becomes compounded by his later failures.

How can we help? I suggest some milestones of helping.

1. Through an understanding of normal development.
2. By motivating the baby and his parents.
3. By interpreting for the baby if necessary.
4. By helping the family to respond gently to him when he has a severe sensory loss.
5. By helping them to talk to him at every opportunity.
6. By helping to fit him into the family.

The knowledge of normal development is vital. But even more important is the final skill. It could be a mistake to bend the child's progress too closely to normal, if this jeopardises the end result. If you consider the skill of holding a pencil, you also recognise that the ultimate aim of writing is to communicate; and in the event, this may have to be by typing, by signing, as with Paget Gorman, or by using Bliss symbols. The understanding and the sharing of the symbol is more important than how it is expressed.

The young baby, up to about two years old, will hold a pencil in a palmar grasp (Fig. 1), and gradually this is transformed into the mature, tripod grasp (Fig. 2) present around $3\frac{1}{2}$–4 years.

Mary is a little girl with no fingers, so an orthopaedic surgeon made her a cleft in her better hand, and she can now write with it, as well as feed and help to dress herself (Figs 3, 4).

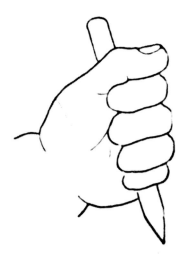

FIG. 1

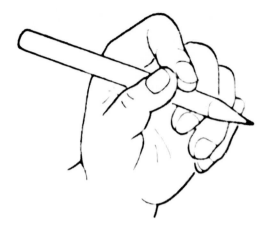

Fig. 2

So the stages of development are important, but more important still, are the goals to aim for. With normal children, the developmental stages are sometimes scarcely recognised, for the child moves forward so quickly. Where a child is seriously handicapped, not only may the stages be seen, but these may be broken down further, and this may provide useful clues to ways of promoting development.

Whatever the child's handicap, motivation is usually needed. This is particularly true for the retarded child whose mother may be heard to say: "He was always so good, I scarcely knew I had him." How can a child be motivated particularly by parents who are often disappointed, depressed, and may have lost confidence in themselves? The teacher can help by valuing the child for himself, by trying to persuade him, enticing him to look, to listen, to respond, by a larger-than-life, warm approach, telling him that it is HE who is loved. And if the baby is switched on, the parents will soon follow.

The teacher may need to interpret for the baby, particularly in terms of normal development. Because she knows about the permanence of objects, she knows that around seven to eight months of age, children become suddenly selective. They now *know* that Mum, whom they cannot see, is somewhere and they may yell until they find her. An adoring Granny may be no alternative, but an explanation always helps. The handicapped child will experience this same intellectual breakthrough at a later date in all probability, or even in a different way, but mothers will learn to accept as a normal stage some behaviour which they feared was aberrant.

FIG. 3

FIG. 4

Gentleness of handling needs a little explanation. It has nothing to do with rough and tumble or the exciting father play which children adore, and handicapped children need as much as others. I mean rather the approach to the child, lying in his cot. For instance, the deaf baby will not hear his mother come into the room, and he may be very frightened if he is suddenly picked up. She needs to go round into his gaze before touching him. The mother of a blind baby will talk to him first, and then touch him gently before picking him up. Even if he seems too young to understand, she can tell him what movement to expect.

The mother of the deaf/blind baby needs all her ingenuity. As well as a very special touch which means Mummy, and another for Daddy, she may use a particular perfume, or one specially fragrant soap, so the baby will become aware of her presence, and get excited at being picked up, as a normal, sighted, hearing child would do (Freeman, 1975).

For the parents to talk to their child may not be easy when they are tired and depressed with lack of progress. We saw earlier that the year-old baby had an idea of a general property we might call 'cupness'—in other words, CUP means much more than just his own individual cup. He still cannot say the word 'cup', but when he does, perhaps around 16 months, he will have heard the word, hopefully in context, at least 500 times. How many more times must the retarded child hear it, so why not start straight away?

Right from the beginning, babies need language about their daily, everyday world, linked to daily everyday objects and their uses.

Lastly, the family who can truly accept their handicapped child, will give him his share, no more, no less, of family concern, though he may for his own needs require more attention. Hopefully, the parents will also delight in him as they do in their other children. A skilled social worker can be of immense help here.

I would now like to mention a few specific ways in which the children may be helped. The deaf child must learn about communication as early as possible, and if he is receiving sound, every effort must be made to link that sound to the words spoken by his mother.

From normal development, we know that around three to five months of age the baby gets 'fixed' on faces. He gazes at you with that devastating look which dries up baby talk; if you smile at him, his response is rapturous. This is the moment to reinforce with deaf babies. If they realise that the sound comes from the mouth, and the mother can keep the child's eyes fixed on to her face, then he is already half-way to lip-reading. And in order to keep him watching her, not just now, but always, she has to learn to make her face as expressive as possible, and make his contact with her very rewarding (Ewing and Ewing, 1971).

The blind baby needs warmth and welcome in the voice that speaks to him; he needs to explore textures and shapes; someone said that the mother of a blind baby should be like a Christmas tree, so he will explore her beads, the texture of her dress, her skin. He needs to be surrounded by an "interesting space" so when his hand accidentally hits at something in front of him, he is curious and encouraged to explore further. There are ingenious mobiles designed to stimulate this sort of play in blind babies (Sokolow and Urwin, 1976).

Mothers of blind babies sometimes despair because the months go by and their babies do not reach to sound, neither do they walk or crawl. The awful thought comes—"Is my baby deaf, or retarded, as well as being blind?" But the teacher can explain this, because in order to reach to sound, the baby has a few intellectual hurdles to put behind him. We talked about the permanence of objects. The ball that has rolled out of sight still exists even though it cannot be seen. In normal babies this comes around seven to eight months, not suddenly but you can watch it happening, in a gradual and wonderful way. At this point, the child will turn to every sound, however quiet, so he can visually confirm what he hears.

For the normal baby, there is no need to understand about permanence of objects in order to reach. He sees something he wants, he has developed good eye/hand coordination, and he reaches out. This may be at six months.

But our blind baby cannot see something he wants—the visual pathway is blocked. If he is instead to reach to sound, he must be aware that there is something to reach towards. In other words, he has understood about permanence of objects. So the teacher can assure the parent that there is nothing unusual when a blind baby reaches to sound apparently late. He needs to take an immense intellectual step before he can do what a sighted child needs only to have eye/hand coordination for. Of course, once he has made that step, he can put some organisation into the darkness of the world around him, and he will soon start moving towards interesting sounds as well (Fraiberg, 1971).

Hands are important for all babies, but for the blind they need to be the bridge between the baby's self and his outside world. If he is to use his hands truly, and communicate with them, he has to be aware of an object world outside himself, however rudimentary. The normal baby brings his hands to midline around four months of age. He then finds that playing with them in his line of vision begins to bring the world into binocular focus. The blind baby has no such rewards for his efforts, so his mother will bring his hands into midline for him, cupping her hands around his, while together they explore shapes, and textures, helping the baby to discover his toes, and find himself in space.

Hand function is something which can be encouraged very success-fully in retarded children. The final aim is to achieve precise finger movements under the control of the eyes. Children with Down's syndrome can be identified early as being in need of help, and if they are well stimulated by their parents in the early years, they may remain close to their 'normal' developmental level for most of their pre-school years.

A programme leading to eye/hand coordination starts with the baby fixing his gaze on his mother's face; later on a toy, which he will learn to follow around. Soon, there may appear a momentary link between the toy which the baby regards, and his hand which may move as though to say, "There is some connection, but I'm not yet sure what that is." Later the hand will go out to the toy and probably miss it; still later, the baby will reach and grasp and now eye and hand work marvellously together for the future. At every step in his progress, the retarded child can be motivated, and rewarded for his efforts, so he is encouraged to make the next step forward (Rosenbaum et al., 1975).

We saw earlier how object permanence comes around seven months. The normal baby devises his own games of Peep-bo and hiding toys, in order to confirm his remarkable discovery that things still exist even if out of sight—the dilemma of the Philosopher's Table. A brick hidden under a cup is a favourite game, with the child picking up the cup with glee to find what he thought he knew would be underneath. The child who is slow may need special help. The game can be shown to the child several times; the cup can be transparent, later more opaque so he still has a clue as to what is inside. But when the game has been played many many times, the retarded child will finally be as sure of the concept of permanence of objects as any of his nimbler brothers (Seifert, 1973).

The last thing I want to mention is language. "Language is called the garment of thought", said Carlyle. We see children who we know are of normal intelligence from their developmental performance in other fields, but they have little speech, and what is worse, little lan-guage. A child needs speech to organise his actions. Luria calls it a directive–integrative function of speech; we have all heard children describing what they are doing, and helpfully, what they plan to do (Luria, 1961).

But those children whose speech and language does not develop deteriorate intellectually. Many of them have switched off to the human voice because they found it harsh and unrewarding. Such children, and there are many of them in the deprived inner city areas, need all the intimacy of a one-to-one programme which I have tried to describe. Language has to be fed in constantly on a day to day, 'life at home' level. Every time they have a drink, the mother talks about the cup, and about drinking from a cup. She will feel the rewards are worth the slight sense of unease she may have at talking in this way. Of course, with many of these children, the opportunity for mother/baby to react in language development may be poor, and we urgently need special classes attached to nursery schools or day nurseries, where skilled teachers and speech therapists can help these children before the intellectual damage has occurred. Otherwise these children will help to swell the numbers of those who are in need of special education at school age.

I have tried to show how a teacher, based on the Child Development Centre, can help parents of handicapped children, to teach these children along known developmental pathways, and to devise other ways for them to progress, if these are needed. These parents become, as so many already are, the expert teachers of the future, who in their turn may pass on their experience to others. Perhaps, who knows, the professionals may find themselves out of a job?

There is also something else about handicapped children of great importance to all doctors and social workers alike, concerning Down's children in particular. The 'mongol' as we know him from our textbooks bears as much resemblance to the Down's child of today as the hydrocephalic child does to the valve-preserved child of modern technology (whatever his future problems may be).

The old-fashioned mongol is a product not of his 47th chromosome but of institutional walls, changing caretakers, lack of stimulation—in fact, lack of loving, family care.

The parents of Down's children have moved with the times. They have children whom they love and who are as rewarding as 'normal' children. They know they will not win academic rewards but they also know that early training in skill of hand, in concentration, in basic learning, will make for job satisfaction in the future. In Spain, severely retarded people do beautiful silk-screen printing and book binding worthy of a skilled craftsman—why? Because they are skilled craftsmen, and have been taught to be.

I suggest that the message given too often by obstetricians and paediatricians at the bedside of a mother, newly delivered of her exceptional baby, is altogether too gloomy, too subjective and based upon past knowledge and past experience. Instead, let them tell the mother that her child is different, that he will need special help with learning, that he will not scale the intellectual heights but he will be as loving, as loved, and as rewarding to his family as any other child.

References

Bradshaw, J. (1977). Services that miss their mark and leave families in need. *Health and Social Services Journal*, April 15.

Ewing, Sir A. and Ewing, Lady (1971). *Hearing-Impaired Children under Five.* Manchester University Press.

Fraiberg, S. (1971). Intervention in infancy: a program for blind infants. *Journal of the American Academy of Child Psychiatry*, **10**, 381–405.

Freeman, P. (1975). *Understanding the Deaf/Blind Child.* London: Heinemann.

Luria, A. R. (1961). *The Role of Speech in the Regulation of Normal and Abnormal Behaviour.* Oxford: Pergamon Press.

Reynell, J. (1976). Early education for handicapped children. *Child Care, Health and Development*, **2**, 305–316.

Rosenbaum, P., Barnitt, R. and Brand, H. L. (1975). A developmental intervention programme designed to overcome the effects of impaired movement in spina bifida infants. In *Movement and Child Development*, edited by K. Holt, Chapter XII. London:-Heinemann.

Seifert, A. (1973). Sensory motor stimulation for the young handicapped child. *Occupational Therapy*, **36**, 559–566.

Sokolow, A. and Urwin, C. (1976). "PlayMobile" for blind infants. *Developmental Medicine and Child Neurology*, **18**, 498–502.

Genetic Disorders: Their Impact on the Family

A. R. BOON

Department of Human Genetics
University of Newcastle upon Tyne, England

This review traces the various ways in which the birth of a child with a genetic disorder subsequently affects the life of the whole family. Such disorders vary in severity, and while the effects may be minimal in the less severe, in others they may be profound. This is demonstrated by reference to conditions of differing modes of inheritance, in which of course the patients' names and locations have been altered to preserve anonymity.

Sex-linked Disorders

Annie Smith was a remarkable grandmother. Not only had she reared a haemophilic son, she had also taken on the responsibility for the care and upbringing of her daughter's son who was also a haemophiliac. One could only assume that this was her way of compensating for the guilt which is so often felt by the mothers who themselves are the carriers of an X-linked disease, and produce an affected son; the deleterious gene has little if any medical effect on such a mother, but any of her sons has a 50 per cent risk of being affected and any of her daughters a similar risk of being a carrier.

Annie Smith came from a large family in the Teesside area and the history of the 'Bleeding Disease' could be traced back to 1820 (Fig. 1). In fact she wrote a letter to her son describing how her grandfather, a brass moulder by trade, was affected by the disease. He died at the age of 45 from a cerebral haemorrhage, but she recounts in vivid detail the frequent swelling of his joints so that he was unable to walk and how he was wheeled about on a hand cart. He fathered at least eight children of whom four had died young (two daughters and two sons). Of the

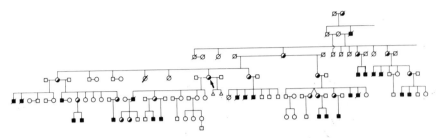

F IG. 1. The haemophilia family.

remaining four children there were three carrier daughters, of whom two produced affected sons. Mrs Smith's mother was one of these carrier daughters and from two marriages she produced three carrier daughters by her first partner, and one carrier by her second husband. In all she was responsible for 17 haemophilic grandsons and greatgrandsons. The mode of inheritance was only realised by the family when it was explained to them after Mrs Smith's sister produced her first affected son.

FAMILY PLANNING

In the days before family planning became generally accepted, these carrier mothers appeared to have had a strong maternal instinct for many produced large families, possibly because of the early deaths among their sons. During the past twenty years contraception has ceased to be a taboo subject, more and more families have become aware of the mode of inheritance and, once an affected son is born to a carrier in the family and the high risk of further affected males is explained to the parents, the obviously desirable family limitation is usually accepted. In Annie Smith's family, in the last ten to fifteen years all the known carriers have requested sterilisation. Details of contraceptive practice were included in a haemophilia survey con-

TABLE I
Haemophilia and contraception

	Numbers Sterilized	Contraceptive pill	Condom	Diaphragm	CI. rhythm or no precautions	Widow or menopause
Mothers of adults (23)	0	2	3	2	1	15
Mothers of children (45)	16	13	4	0	9	5

ducted in north-east England in 1968 (Boon and Roberts, 1970) which provided the data for this review. The results showed a remarkable increase in sterilisation among the mothers of the younger affected males (Table I), from 0 to 34 per cent.

PARENTAL REACTION

The age of diagnosis is usually at the toddler stage. If there is a family history the mother may already be aware of the risks, but the shock of the diagnosis is always profound and especially so in a family where the disease has arisen as a new mutation. The expressions which were constantly repeated by mothers during the survey were 'disbelief, dismay, horror and anxiety'. In time the parents come to accept the situation and the mothers adapt more readily to the problems than do the fathers.

TREATMENT

In this they are greatly helped by the change in medical treatment over the years which has been remarkable. Earlier in this century rest in bed and splinting of the limbs was all that could be done. Prolonged stay in hospital was sometimes necessary. Then blood transfusions and later plasma transfusions were found to arrest the bleeding, but again hospital admission was necessary. Intravenous injection of cryo-precipitate was introduced about 1967 and patients could then be treated on an outpatient basis. Finally freeze dried factor VIII is now the treatment of choice and can be given in the home. The reason is that the more rapidly a bleed is brought under control the less severe is its effects. The effects of this changed pattern of treatment are far reaching. More and more responsibility has devolved upon the parents of an affected boy and they are required to achieve a considerable degree of skill in giving the intravenous injections, and of course the mother is still required to give constant supervision and attention. Unless she has a good substitute (perhaps her mother or sister), there is little chance of her going out to work until the boy has left school, and the deprivation in terms of interest and finance, and hence social amenities, is keenly felt though not necessarily complained of. However, the most important effect of the changed treatment is that today there is a minimum of time lost by the patient from school and work. This was not so in the past when recurrent hospital admissions often meant prolonged absences from school. Many boys attended schools for the physically handicapped, but for others their education was repeatedly interrupted: few reached advanced levels of education. The scope of employment open to them was therefore greatly limited. Similarly adults found it difficult to hold a job on account of repeated absences, and certainly through no fault of their own.

SOCIAL RELATIONS

In most families the affected boy is accepted by the other children who are encouraged to care for him, but there were two exceptions in the survey of 45 child haemophiliacs where the boy caused difficulties and friction within the family. Family holidays are curtailed to some extent, either for financial reasons or for deliberate restriction of travelling because of uncertainty of the health of the haemophiliac. Camping or caravaning within easy access of a treatment centre was the choice of seven families in the survey while others stayed with relatives.

Recessive Disorders

Cystic fibrosis has the highest incidence of all the autosomal recessive disorders and it is estimated that 1 in 20 of the population carries the gene for this defect. Both parents of an affected child are heterozygous carriers of the disease and therefore there is a 1 in 4 chance that any further child they produce will be similarly affected.

Since it is a recessive disorder both parents are normal and it is unusual to find a positive family history in earlier generations. This being so, the family of each parent is apt to blame that of the other; the grandparents are equally adamant that there is no hereditary disease in 'their' family. Here the way in which the parents are told about the condition and its inheritance has a profound effect.

FAMILY LIFE

It is not only for family cohesion that the way of telling the news is important. Parents must be encouraged from the start to think and act positively concerning the disease so that, for example, they can deal with dietary restrictions and combat respiratory infections as far as possible. The disease, in fact, becomes a way of life for the whole family. In the early days the bulky offensive motions in the baby's nappy entail extra work for the mother. So does the careful supervision of the diet, and in particular the food supplements (pancreatic extract which is unpalatable to young children) which may cause trouble at mealtimes, but to this the young patients are more amenable when the diagnosis is made at an early age. There are the additional demands on the mother's time by the need for physiotherapy to clear the bronchi which has to be undertaken night and morning.

Family life is affected both within and outside the home. Protection against infection may curtail activities. The family needs to avoid crowds, cinemas, public transport and children's parties and other situations where infection may be transmitted, while fog and inclement weather may prevent attendance at school. Family holidays are likewise affected. Travel abroad is difficult because of diet, the problem of hospital treatment, and inability to withstand the hotter climates—due to salt depletion. Smoking needs to be discouraged in the home and visitors asked not to indulge in the habit when visiting.

Educational problems arise. As with haemophilia, schooling may be interrupted or curtailed, and the child penalised when the examination stage is reached. Suitable employment may be difficult to find and the parents need to give the problem much thought while the child is young in order to equip him suitably to enjoy as normal a life as possible.

GENETIC COUNSELLING

Genetic counselling is important, both as regards their own further reproduction and the implications for their children. The parents' response to counselling on the genetic basis of cystic fibrosis was studied in Edinburgh by McRae and others (1973) in 50 Scottish and 50 Irish families. The results showed:

(a) Poor education and intellectual ability of parents, factors that make it particularly difficult for them to cope adequately with the affected child.

(b) Lack of understanding of the nature of the genetic disease and this leads to unhappiness, depression and guilt. This was partly due to bad timing of the counselling, which took place too soon after the initial diagnosis when its message was lost in the parental shock at the severity of the disease and concern at its management.

FAMILY PLANNING

A particularly clear feature to emerge from the Edinburgh survey was the inadequacy of instruction in birth control. Although in 20 of the families in which no further children were intended one partner had been sterilised, in 18 there had occurred accidental pregnancies out of which there were 3 miscarriages and 4 terminations; but of the 11 pregnancies going to term there was fortunately only one affected child. In the 26 families who decided to have further children there were seven affected children. In many families the fathers had not been seen, and they did not understand the high recurrence risk or mode of inheritance, or that family planning was necessary. In the lower socio-economic groups the parents did not discuss family planning with each other and in fact only one-third of the sample had discussed birth control with a doctor.

From the assessment of understanding of the inheritance of cystic fibrosis, it also emerged that few parents realised that their affected sons are likely to be sterile, and that all affected girls would produce only carriers whose spouses could also unknowingly be carriers (1 in 20 of them) and therefore in turn could produce affected children.

MARITAL STRESS

A handicapped child may draw the parents closer together, but this is not necessarily the case. Out of the 50 Scottish cystic fibrosis families there was one divorce and 8 broken marriages and, although the defect in the child was said not to be entirely responsible for the marital break-up (Table II), comparable figures in other groups of families show that the rate of broken homes is considerably higher in cystic fibrosis families. The potential fragility of such unions is a sound reason not to advise sterilisation when the parents are under 30 years of age; they may decide to separate, and re-marriage of each would then produce different genetic combinations with much lower risk of this condition to offspring in the new unions.

The difficulties consequent upon too rapid sterilisation are well illus-

TABLE II
The effect on marital stability following the birth of a handicapped child

Condition	Number of families in survey	Number where no further children planned	Sterilised M	F	Separated or Divorced
Haemophilia	46	?		16	1
Cystic fibrosis	50	36	2	10	9
Fallot's tetralogy	100	53	1	6	4
Controls	47	14		2	0

trated in the family of Charles and Mary Fitch (Fig. 2). They were aged 27 and 24 and unrelated, and were referred to the genetic counselling service by a health visitor attached to a group practice because she was concerned about the marital stress following the birth and death of two children with cystic fibrosis. The young parents married in 1969. Their first child born in 1970 is said to be 'chesty' but otherwise normal. An early spontaneous abortion followed in 1972, and in 1973

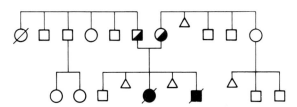

F IG. 2. The cystic fibrosis family.

the first affected child was born and died at the age of twelve days. The following year there was another ten-week abortion, after which the mother immediately became pregnant again and the second affected child was born in 1976. He developed a meconium ileus and was operated upon, but died aged four months. Both the paediatrician and surgeon concerned with this case suggested that the father should be sterilised and, without careful explanation of the genetic aspects of the disease and full discussion of the implications, a vasectomy was performed.

When the mother was seen for genetic counselling it emerged that:

(a) The parents were not aware that they were both carriers of the deleterious gene, and that this was the reason for the high 1 in 4 risk of an affected child in any pregnancy. They did not appreciate therefore that if either partner had an accident and the other wished to re-marry the genetic risk would be quite different.

(b) They had not appreciated that a vasectomy was irreversible and therefore Charles would never be able to produce further children.

After the death of the second child the father had attempted suicide and the mother had a nervous breakdown. Any attempt at discussion of their problems led to furious arguments between the couple. The father in fact refused to attend the counselling session; he was working on the night shift in a factory and the mother was working during the day so that the couple had very little time together. Artificial insemination had been discussed but the husband was not agreeable, and in any case this is not readily available in the north-east, even if the legal aspects were clarified. The alternatives of adoption or fostering had also been raised, but again Charles was not agreeable; in any case with the unstable background they are unlikely to be regarded as suitable adoptive parents. The psychological effects of the vasectomy have left him feeling totally inadequate and no longer a man, so it may be some time before he will be able to come to terms with their family problems.

Polygenic Disorders

Congenital heart disease is not simply inherited as in the previous examples, for development of the heart is controlled by a number of genes which in turn may be affected by the environment. The effects of congenital heart disease on the family can be illustrated by one condition, Fallot's tetralogy, of which a recent survey was made (Boon, 1972).

The age of diagnosis in this condition is variable according to the severity of the lesion, the majority of cases being diagnosed between one and four months when the parents have had time to become attached to the baby (Boon *et al.*, 1972). It thus differs from transposition of the great arteries which is usually diagnosed within hours or days after birth, and from coarctation of the aorta which may not be diagnosed for months or years. Obviously if the baby is blue at birth, has breathing and feeding difficulties, the parents suspect at an early age that all is not well. Some doctors do not tell the parents the nature of the problem in the early stages and some intelligent parents are resentful if explanations are withheld.

PARENTAL REACTION

Since congenital heart disease is usually, but not always, an isolated congenital defect in the family, the parents have no reason to suspect that the child may be born with a flaw in the heart. When the parents are told of the condition, the same expressions of disbelief and shock are encountered. "Why should it happen to us?" is asked repeatedly. Many have difficulty in understanding the gravity of the condition and nature of the defect and are grateful for a full discussion of their problems.

The subsequent effect on the family is most marked when there are other children to look after, for this increases the mental, physical and financial stress involved and the parents remark on it repeatedly. Until recently children from north-east England with severe congenital heart disease had to travel to London for operative treatment; with an adequate paediatric cardiology service in the region now this problem has been alleviated to some extent, though still a journey from home to the regional centre perhaps 50 miles distant may be a major undertaking for repeated hospital visits. But other problems arise when there are no other children. When the proband is an only child he lacks companionship and has difficulty making friends due to his inability to join in normal activities. There is a tendency for parents to 'spoil' these children in order to avoid cyanotic attacks brought on by temper tantrums. Great skill and patience is required of the parents in the sensible management of these children.

The repercussions in one family were interesting where the ten-year-old child with Fallot's tetralogy was also mentally retarded. She attended a junior day centre, the father (a draftsman) arranged to do some of his desk work at home and the mother took a part-time job. In this way one of the parents was always at home to be available if the child was ill or on holiday from school, and at the same time each was able to get out of the house for a period each day and enjoy the benefit of another environment. In general in these cases, however, the mother's work and recreation outside the house is severely curtailed until the child has received surgical treatment and started school.

FAMILY BUILDING

Of the 100 Fallot families in the survey, 53 had no further children after the propositus was born; 12 mothers expressed a wish to have a further pregnancy, and six decided to postpone the event until the affected child's health improved. Evidence for similar postponement in the other families comes from the finding that the average interval between the affected child and the next pregnancy was 3 years and 7 months compared with 2 years 11 months in a matched control group of children. Sterilisation is not resorted to as frequently as in the single gene disorders, for there was only a slight increase in the number of mothers sterilised in the affected group compared with the controls. There was no evidence of a period of infertility or of interrupted pregnancies immediately preceding the birth of the index case.

There is no doubt that following successful surgery the psychological outlook for the whole family is changed for the better. The children become more active physically and, due to an improved appetite and circulation, they start to grow more rapidly. The mothers are no longer burdened with a physically handicapped child and are free to lead a more independent life, many taking a part-time job as soon as circumstances permit. No operation can be undertaken without some risk to the life of the patient, but as surgical techniques become safer the mortality rate of about 10 per cent in these cases should be reduced.

Case Histories

Besides such surveys of series of cases, individual family case histories provide useful illustrations of the types of problem, social rather than biological, that are encountered, and there are a number among the many interesting family problems coming to the Newcastle Genetic Service over the course of the past ten years which are worth recording. For example:

Case 1
There is a family well-known to us whose members suffer from the dominantly inherited dystonia musculorum deformans (Fig. 3).

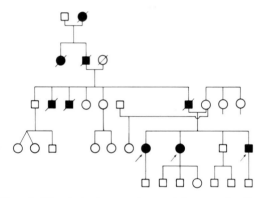

Fɪɢ. 3. The dystonia muculorum deformans family.

Onset of the disease is in early adult life with painful spasm and dystonic movements in the limbs, which may spread to the trunk and also involve speech. Within ten years of onset the patient is usually confined to a wheelchair. The patient usually has had children before the onset.

Emily R., the mother of the three affected patients was divorced from their father soon after the onset of symptoms in him during World War II. He left the area and lived in a Salvation Army hostel in Hammersmith and subsequently died from 'paralysis' in West Sussex. Other relatives in the father's family who were traced were thought to have had Huntington's chorea but since they did not suffer from choreiform movements or dementia it is more likely that they also had the dystonia. In the meantime Mrs R. remarried, had a normal daughter by her second husband, and all her other children changed their surname to that of their stepfather.

Her affected offspring now aged 39, 38 and 33 have all been married and produced children, but the two daughters are now both divorced. They all live within walking distance of each other but Mrs R. now aged 65 is the mainstay of the family. She maintains a part-time job, and with the aid of a friend she does all the shopping, cooking and gardening for the three households. The cooking is organised in the older daughter's house and sometimes ten members of the family assemble for meals. Each individual is encouraged to help in some way despite the severe handicap; for instance they all wash their own dishes. The affected son, knowing the hereditary nature of the disease, elected to have a vasectomy recently. He has one boy of 7 years and the children of the two affected women are in their teens. These 5 children each have a 50 per cent risk of inheriting this crippling disease, from the three affected parents, and had genetic counselling been available twenty years ago some of the problems arising in this family might have been averted. But it illustrates clearly the spirit of independence that occurs in so many families, the desire to cope by themselves without being a burden to society, and the great strains on a marriage that such late onset disorders impose.

Case 2

Norma and Tom were newly married and very anxious to start a family. They were referred for genetic counselling and at first sight the future looked depressing (Fig. 4).

Norma (24) was deaf from birth and as a result had never been able to talk. She can read and write, lip read and use sign language. At the

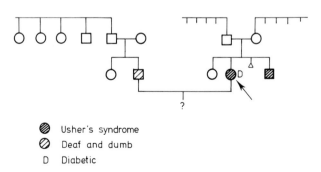

● Usher's syndrome
⊘ Deaf and dumb
D Diabetic

FIG. 4. The Usher's syndrome family.

age of 16 she was found to be diabetic and about the same time her vision began to fail, and a diagnosis of retinitis pigmentosa was made. The combination of deaf mutism and retinitis pigmentosa is recognised as Usher's syndrome, which is inherited as an autosomal recessive condition. Norma has a brother with the same defect. Norma's husband, Tom, is also a deaf mute. Investigation in his case, however, indicated that the condition was caused by meningitis at 14 months of age, and conclusive proof that he was not affected by Usher's syndrome was obtained by electroretinogram examination.

We were therefore able to reassure the couple that their conditions were different and that there was a negligible risk of deafness occurring in any children they produced. However, the early onset of diabetes in Norma carries a 1 in 10 risk that her children may also develop diabetes and this risk they were prepared to accept. At the same time we gave them some idea of the likely future of Norma's vision. They decided to start a family while there was still time for her to enjoy and learn to cope with the offspring. As soon as these aspects were clarified Norma became pregnant.

Because of the nature of their disabilities it was preferable to see them in domiciliary interviews. At the initial interview it was realised that the couple had considerable social problems. They were living in a rented upstairs flat, with a steep stairway to an outside W.C. and no bathroom, with a half hour's journey to the nearest relative. While her husband was out working, Norma, no longer able to work, was left on her own all day. Her mother also worked from 9 a.m. to 3 p.m., and there was no one to supervise the treatment for her diabetes.

This was clearly an unsatisfactory situation. We therefore made contact with the Aids Centre of the Council for the Disabled in Newcastle and as a result, and with help from a local Housing Association, the couple were rehoused in a bungalow within easy reach of her mother and married sister.

The problems in this family had not been met by the welfare services, partly because of their nature, partly because of their complexity. There were a number of distinct yet interlocking questions which required coordination, and in this instance the genetic advisory service was in a position to do this:

(a) Assess and advise on the hereditary risk attaching to the deafness, blindness, muteness and diabetes.
(b) Appreciate the problems of managing a young diabetic with the added complication of close supervision required during pregnancy.

(c) Coordinate with the family doctor the provision of regular Health Visitor liaison with the family.

(d) Appreciate the difficulties of the original accommodation for those disabled like Norma and Tom, and make recommendations on the need for rehousing and the premises required.

(e) Advise about aids for the disabled.

(f) Advise about family planning acceptable to them.

The rehousing was achieved before the baby was born. The bungalow moreover was equipped with essential aids: for example the door bell produced a flashing light in all main rooms; a visual intercom system was installed, with sound from the baby's room producing a flashing light in the kitchen, living room and parents' bedroom.

The child, a healthy boy, is now 9 months old. He can hear and is developing normally both mentally and physically. He is stimulated by hearing voices on the radio and TV and daily visits from his grandmother, aunt and small cousins. The couple are proving to be capable and very proud and loving parents.

So far everything has gone well for this handicapped couple since referral to the Genetic Service and hopefully Norma will not lose her sight completely before she has had the joy of rearing a family.

Conclusion

The genetic defects which have been discussed in this paper impose upon the families involved problems which may be far reaching. Despite the very different nature of the conditions illustrated, there is a consistency about the problems that emerge. They may be complex and require a coordinated approach, and this is one of the reasons why they may all too easily slip through the meshes of the welfare services' net, efficient though this is in dealing with specific problems. Another reason is the independence and self-reliance of so many of the families.

All cases are referred to hospital sooner or later for diagnosis, assessment and treatment, which may involve numerous visits for constant supervision and this may prove a strain on family life, both financial and otherwise. In those families where there is a known hereditary component there is frequently a guilt complex on the part of the carriers, whether it be a sex-linked, recessive, or dominant condition. The shock to the parents, when the diagnosis is made in childhood, and to the patient when made later in life, is profound, requires to be recognised and managed. The patient's nursing or treatment at home may be intensely worrying. Intense too may be the concern about education, ultimate employment and his ability to lead a normal life. With the passage of time comes the realisation of the constrictions placed on family life. With these superimposed on the worry regarding the hereditary aspects of the disease, is there any wonder that a proportion of families disintegrate?

Clear and adequate contraceptive advice is almost always desirable; genetic counselling when the mode of inheritance and recurrence risk and the reasons for it can be explained slowly and sympathetically is a useful follow-up for the parents with a handicapped child and is particularly important in forestalling intrafamilial recriminations. In this way the shock to the parents may be alleviated to some extent, particularly if it is a condition which can be detected antenatally.

Some of the problems in these families which have been mentioned may only become apparent through the genetic advisory service, and it is often necessary to coordinate help with the social services and family doctors. This is not to say that their roles are subsumed, but it is our experience that our colleagues are grateful for the information made available to them, and mutual cooperation has been excellent.

Genetic advisory centres are few in number at present, but this is a rapidly growing branch of modern medicine and it is important that the day-to-day problems of the individual and family unit should be considered with as much care as the rapidly increasing knowledge in the scientific field of genetics.

References

Boon, A. R. (1972). Tetralogy of Fallot—effect on the family. *British Journal of Preventive and Social Medicine*, **26**, 263–268.

Boon, A. R., Farmer, M. B. and Roberts, D. F. (1972). A family study of Fallot's tetralogy. *Journal of Medical Genetics*, **9**, 179–192.

Boon, A. R. and Roberts, D. F. (1970). The social impact of haemophilia. *Journal of Biosocial Science*, **2**, 237–264.

McCrae, W. M., Cull, A. M., Burton, L. and Dodge, J. (1973). Cystic fibrosis: the parents' response to the genetic basis of disease. *The Lancet*, **ii**, 141–143.

Patterns of Mortality and the Alienation of Life: A Study using Census Indicators

MARY E. BRENNAN

West Midlands Regional Health Authority, Birmingham, England

Introduction

Although the overall mortality has dropped substantially in this country during the past twenty-five years, there still remain large differences in the rate between different socio-economic groups.

Recent work has demonstrated that there is still a positive gradient between socio-economic position and mortality. Lambert (1976) has clearly demonstrated that although overall absolute mortality has fallen, the mortality decrease is much less in social class V compared with social class I. Adelstein and White (1976) have shown that for the age-group 1–4 years the rate is more than doubled from social class I as defined by the Registrar-General to social class V. In the age-group 5–9 years, a similar effect occurs and in the age-group 10–14 years the increase is over a third. However, socio-economic status may only be an indicator of other types of deprivation and its use as a sole indicator may be misleading (*British Medical Journal*, 1976).

In an interesting study thirty years ago (Woolfe and Waterhouse, 1945) it was shown that infant mortality was related to unemployment, low pay and overcrowding. These results were disbelieved at the time and the contention of the authors that the infant mortality rate among deprived groups could be reduced using the medical techniques of that time to a figure of just above 20 from over 100, was regarded as ridiculous. This aim has recently been achieved, but there still remains differences in the rate between various socio-economic groups.

This paper sets out to examine the association of socio-economic factors and mortality in adult life including housing density, the use of amenities and the proportion of unemployed. It examines whether any association is maintained when the effect of social class is kept at a constant level. A paper describing the results for infants is being published elsewhere.

Since socio-economic data directly from individual income and housing status are often difficult to obtain and are unreliable, a geographical analysis using census data from county boroughs in England has been undertaken. This method has been shown to have several advantages (Simon, 1974) and although the administrative areas concerned did not present entirely homogeneous socio-economic characteristics within each borough, sufficient variation occurred between them to explore the socio-economic mechanisms involved.

Method

The mortality rates for various age-groups were obtained from the Registrar-General for each county borough in England except the City of London, which was excluded, for 1971. Information was collated from the 1971 Census to provide information for each county borough on the following characteristics as defined by that source.

Socio-economic factors included:

(a) housing density: the percentage living with one person and over per room of living space,
(b) amenities: the percentage with no hot water, no bath, no inside toilet, enjoying exclusive use of amenities, and
(c) tenure, i.e. percentages of owner occupiers and council house tenants.

Various employment indicators were also collated including the proportion of unemployed respondents.

The average rating value for domestic establishments for each county borough was also obtained from the report of the Municipal Treasurers. The proportion of the population aged 15–64 years in social classes I, IV and V was also obtained from the census. The definitions used were the standard ones employed by the Registrar-General.

A rank correlation technique was used to ascertain which socio-economic factors had an independent association at different age groups. Each variable was ranked for one to 111 according to the relevant factor for each county borough and Kendall's rank correlation coefficient was then computed to determine the association between mortality rates at specific ages and the factor under consideration.

This particular method was chosen instead of the product moment coefficient because it was not likely the relations involved were strictly linear. It also had the additional advantage in that it could be used to determine partial correlation coefficients so that the association between two variables could be measured while a third was then being kept constant. There is every reason to believe that for samples of this size an approximate test of significance using the standard normal distribution should be accurate.

Results

The mortality rates for each age-group is shown in Table I. The London boroughs have lower mortalities than the provinces in both the age-groups categorised in this study, but particularly in the age-group 45–64 years. In the age-group 15–44 years the mean mortality in the provinces was 50·3 per 100,000, with a standard deviation of 12·6, while in London the mean was 43·5 with a standard deviation of 9·5. In the age-group 45–64 years the mean for the provinces was 569·9 per

TABLE I

Average mortality rates for age-groups in adult population for county boroughs in England per 100,000 population of that age-group

Age group	London		Provinces		All	
	rate	standard deviation	rate	standard deviation	rate	standard deviation
15–44 years	43·5	9·1	50·3	12·7	48·3	12·2
45–64 years	462·5	61·1	569·9	103·7	538·9	105·2
Number of boroughs	32		79		111	

100,000 with a standard deviation of 103·7 and for London the mean was 462·5 with a standard deviation of 61·1. There was a substantial variation between boroughs; for instance, for the age-group 15–44 years, Southend-on-Sea had a mortality rate of 22·1 per 100,000 and Dewsbury 104·2 per 100,000 and in the age-group 45–64 years Bath had a mortality rate of 372·3 per 100,000 while that of Preston was 926·8 per 100,000 (Table I).

Mortality in both age-groups is highly correlated with various socio-economic indicators (Tables II and III).

The mortality rate in both age-groups was correlated against the proportion of *social class V men*. There was a positive correlation in both groups at a level of significance of 0·1 per cent. If the boroughs were ranked in order and the mortality rate compared for those boroughs in the top quarter with those in the bottom quarter it was found that the mortality rate was increased by 25 per cent in the age-group 15–44 years and 50 per cent in the age-group 45–64 years.

However, other factors had a significant effect and a high level of significance between the number of *unemployed men* and the mortality rate in both age-groups ($p < 0.001$) was found. The difference in mortality in absolute terms was also computed for different quartiles when boroughs were ranked for unemployment; the range varied from 2·1 per cent in Solihull to 10·6 per cent in Liverpool in 1971. The mean mortality of the highest quartile for the age-group 15–44 years showed

TABLE II

Correlation of various socio-economic indicators with
mortality rates from county boroughs in England (1971)

Variable (as a proportion of total population)	Kendall's rank correlation coefficient	
	15–44 yrs	45–64 yrs
Unemployed respondents	0·233‡	0·429‡
Proportion in Social class I	−0·118 N.S.	−0·429‡
Proportion in Social class IV	0·157*	0·260‡
Proportion in Social class V	0·200†	0·479‡
Average domestic rating per household	−0·100 N.S.	−0·443‡

‡ (p 0·00)   † (p 0·01)   * (p 0·05).

an increase of 22 per cent over the lowest quartile and for the age-group 45–64 years an increase of 40 per cent was demonstrated (Table II).

Using Kendall's rank correlation the associations between various *housing indicators* derived from census data and mortality were also computed (Table III). The results are shown for both age-groups but are more impressive in the older age-group where nearly all the indicators were significant at the 0·1 per cent level.

Density was highly significant in both age-groups. The difference in

TABLE III
Correlation of housing variables derived from census data with mortality rates for county boroughs in England (*1971*)

Variable (as a proportion of total population)	Kendall's rank correlation coefficient	
housing density	15–44 yrs	45–64 yrs
Living 1 or more per room	0·202†	0·376‡
Living 1½ or more per room	0·185†	0·249‡
Exclusive use of amenities	−0·132*	−0·254‡
No hot water	0·087 N.S.	0·251‡
No bath	0·155*	0·424‡
No inside toilet	0·143*	0·486‡
Council house tenants	0·111 N.S.	0·153*

‡ (p < 0·001)   † (p < 0·01)   * (p < 0·05)   N.S. Not significant.

absolute terms was computed for the ranked boroughs in the proportion of households with one or more persons per room. At the lowest quartile point the proportion of the population living in households with one or more persons per room was 8·2 per cent and at the highest quartile was 12·7 per cent. The range varied from 4·6 per cent in Solihull to 18·2 per cent in Tower Hamlets. It was found the mean for the highest quartile was just over a quarter higher than that for the lowest quartile for the younger age-group and a similar percentage (28 per cent) was found for the older age-group.

When partial correlations were computed *eliminating the effect of social class* as indicated by the proportion of the male population in social class V, many of these associations did not then reach a statistically significant level for the younger age-group, thereby demonstrating the importance of socio-economic position in this age-group (Table IV). However, this was not true in the older age-groups where housing conditions had a significant association independent of social class. The association in London was highly significant (*p* < 0·001) even though there was a very high correlation between overcrowding and the indicators of low socio-economic positions.

When the partial correlation was computed for the age-group 45–64 for the association of class (as shown by the proportion of men in class V), with mortality holding the effect of unemployment constant, the effect was eliminated.

The conclusions are that unemployment characteristics in an area have a close association with mortality among younger adults and the

TABLE IV

Correlation of selected housing variables derived from census data with Mortality
Rates for County Boroughs in England (1971) holding a social class indicator
constant for the age-group 15—44 years and 45—64 years

Variable as a proportion of total population	Kendall's rank correlation coefficient with the proportion of social class V	Partial correlation coefficient of mortality with housing indices holding class constant	
		15–44 yrs	45–64 yrs
Living 1 or more per room	0·530‡	0·115 N.S.	0·130†
Exclusive use of amenities	−0·447‡	−0·048 N.S.	−0·019 N.S.
No bath	0·593‡	0·046 N.S.	0·158†
No inside toilet	0·586‡	0·033 N.S.	0·253‡

‡ (p. 0·001)   † (p 0·01)   N.S. Not significant.

housing characteristics have a close association among older adults,
when the effect of social class is eliminated.

Discussion

Man as a species is characterised by an ability to use tools and the use
of speech, both of which reflect the essentially cooperative aspect of
man's activity. The nature and expression of this cooperation is delin-
eated by the social and cultural activity of any community, which is
dialectically related to the technological and socio-economic conditions. However, in certain historical periods the socio-economic conditions do not reflect the technological advances which have occurred
and the resulting social structure inhibits cooperative social relations
and promotes divisive competitive ones. Cooperation and conflict
always co-exist and frequently complement each other, their interaction progressing social production. However, if the social structure of
the community is outmoded and unable to maintain the advances
generated by technology, cooperation is inhibited and social conflict
and struggle predominate, which become destructive if the socio-
economic structure of that society does not reflect the basic changes
which have occurred in technology and culture. In this society where
25 per cent of the population own 90 per cent of the country's wealth
(*Social Trends*, 1975) and the income from profits and investment are
substantially higher than that from pensions (*Social Trends,* 1976),
such a situation probably exists. For in this society with a highly
advanced technology, the social structure promotes unemployment and

perpetuates poor housing and an unacceptably low income level among a substantial proportion of the population. If statistics are analysed by area it can be demonstrated that those in the most socially deprived quarter have a mortality rate between 20 and 50 per cent higher than that of the top quarter. Such a distribution of 'life chances', to use Weber's term, can only promote struggle and conflict eventually, although a period of disinterest and apathy may intervene. As a species, man is only likely to survive if he is able to improve his technology and improve and advance his communication and culture. This progress is unlikely in a society whose inequalities are so marked that they militate against cooperative production. "Man can only save his life by losing it." Certainly in this case the old saying is indeed true.

ACKNOWLEDGEMENTS

I wish to express my gratitude to the technical staff of the Department of Social Medicine, the University of Birmingham, for all their help with the analysis of this material, particularly Mr Robert Lancashire, Senior computer programmer, and also the staff of OPCS, who compiled the data on mortality.

References

Adelstein, A. M. and White, G. (1976). Causes of children's death analysed by social class. In *Child Health, A Collection of Studies*, edited by A. M. Adelstein and others. Studies of Medicine and Population Subjects, No. 31, p. 25. London: HMSO.
British Medical Journal (1976). Leading Article, **ii**, 962.
Lambert, P. (1976). Perinatal trends: social and environmental factors. *Population Trends*, **4**, 4.
Simon, J. L. (1974). *The Effects of Income on Fertility*. Chapel Hill: Carolina Population Center.
Social Trends (1975). No. 6. London: HMSO.
Social Trends (1976). No. 7. London: HMSO.
Woolfe, B. and Waterhouse, J. (1945). Studies of infant mortality. *Journal of Hygiene* **2**, 67.

The Centre–Periphery Model of Educational Inequality: A Critical Assessment

W. WILLIAMSON

Department of Sociology and Social Administration
University of Durham, Durham, England

This paper is written in the belief that nothing is so practical as a good theory. My aim is to urge all those who are concerned with the role educational change may play in bringing about a more equal society to reconsider the basic theoretical presuppositions which inform their work. This may seem a rather presumptuous thing to do but as I shall try and make clear there are good reasons for it. In the uncertain economic climate of the 1970s during a period when public expenditure cuts, inflation and demographic changes have all combined to reduce the likelihood of resources being made available for education there is little room for innovation and experimentation in education policy. In the acrimonious political environment of the 1970s it is equally clear that the optimistic consensus of the 1960s that, somehow, growth and change in education was both necessary and desirable, has finally evaporated. The so-called Great Debate which Prime Minister Callaghan initiated in his Ruskin speech, has brought little other than opportunity for party politicians to score dubious points about educational standards or comprehensive schooling and what might emerge as the most positive outcome of the debate, namely, efforts to link the school curriculum more closely to the needs of the labour market, might, in the end, prove to have been a disaster. The seductions of the labour market are already too attractive to large numbers of school-leavers for the schools to attempt to reinforce them.

But what concerns me most of all in this paper are the terms in which we ought to understand the role which education now plays in our society and the kinds of explanations which are given particularly of the persisting, though changing, problem of educational inequality. For it seems to me that, also in contrast to the 1960s and early 1970s, a mood of unjustifiable pessimism has come to dominate the way in which the educational system itself is analysed. It has become something of an academic dogma that making schools more equal or aiming to make children more equal in their performance at school will do little to make society itself more equal. This point has been made most forcibly by Christopher Jencks and his colleagues (1973) but it has also been made by Raymond Boudon (1973) and even by the Marxist writers S. Bowles and H. Gintis (1976). Each of those referred to make the same point but in different ways and for different reasons, and each invites a re-evaluation of the kinds of assumptions which lay behind educational policy all over western Europe and the United States during the 1960s. In a small way I want to contribute to that re-evaluation in this paper but to stress that it is too premature to write off educational change as an instrument of social change towards a fairer society. To insist, whether from the perspective of a functionalist or a Marxist that the inequalities of society which are reflected in schools must be changed before schools themselves can change, is to suffer from a condition which, following Professor Gouldner (1964) I shall call 'metaphysical pathos'. It is a metaphysical position because it goes beyond the evidence in the case; it is pathetic in that it leads to a kind of political impotence from which only those who already do quite well from the system can benefit.

To clarify my position it is necessary to review the kinds of assumptions which influenced studies of educational inequality in the 1960s and a convenient way of doing this is to highlight some of the key theoretical issues with which many of these studies were preoccupied.

In 1971 David Byrne and I published a paper with the deliberately provocative title *The Myth of the Restricted Code* (Byrne and Williamson, 1971). The paper achieved some notoriety because it brought into question the explanatory power of some currently fashionable theories of educational attainment, particularly theories about language, to explain the well-known social class variations in school attainment. We suggested that cultural theories of educational attainment could not explain the large variation in educational life chances among different social class groups or within such groups. What was of decisive importance, we argued, was the unequal, historically conditioned distribution of resources for education, patterns of educational provision and structures of control. To suggest otherwise is to step across the thin red line which divides scientific observation from ideology.

We followed this work up with a much larger study of local education authorities in England and Wales as a whole, and the results were published in our book *The Poverty of Education* (Byrne *et al.*, 1975). There we argued that a resources/provision of model of educational inequality had a greater explanatory value than a class/culture model. And we concluded that what was necessary, if the educational social income of our society were to be redistributed, was that working-class people, particularly those most disadvantaged should unite, where possible, with radical teachers to demand a fair distribution of resources. The act of doing so we felt might trigger off greater demands which would bring in to question the whole complex structure of inequality which affects their lives.

This book had an academic half-life of about six months and a political life much shorter even than that. In retrospect this is hardly surprising; the book came at a time when the political consensus of the 1960s that growth in education was desirable had ended, when the optimism that educational changes could contribute to broader social changes had burnt out and when the murky crisis in the economy had settled in like dark weather in Wales.

In addition, despite our efforts, it had become something of a commonplace that inequalities in educational opportunity, except, of course, for a number of groups suffering from multiple social handicaps, had their origin in different learning environments in the home and in the community.

My main argument in this paper is that this latter view is at best partial and that it rests upon a broader sociological perspective which might be called the 'centre–periphery model of educational disadvantage'.

As a way of posing questions about inequalities a centre-periphery model can be represented as in figure 1.

The centre of society includes all of those people who, in a conventional way, do quite well at work. They have secure incomes although not necessarily high incomes. Their families are stable and sustain personal growth. Their housing is adequate. They have done quite well at school and their children are performing adequately too. They have all the characteristics of respectable citizenship and they are making adequate provision for old age. The periphery includes all those who are poor and/or inadequate. They may be unemployed. Their family life may have pathological characteristics. They may be badly housed and their children may do badly at school. They often are not capable of ensuring their basic citizenship rights particularly in such areas as entitlements to a range of welfare benefits.

Neither group is, of course, homogenous and the poverties to which

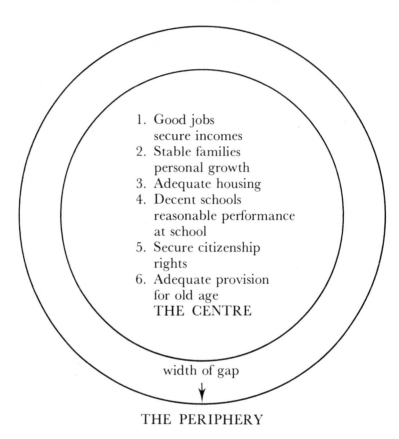

1. Good jobs
   secure incomes
2. Stable families
   personal growth
3. Adequate housing
4. Decent schools
   reasonable performance
   at school
5. Secure citizenship
   rights
6. Adequate provision
   for old age
   THE CENTRE

width of gap

THE PERIPHERY

Fig. 1. The centre–periphery model of educational disadvantage.

the periphery is subjected are complex. But for my present purpose it is
not necessary to elaborate the differences. It is sufficient to note that
from this perspective the assumption is made that if the centre expands
it will gradually incorporate the periphery. A point would then be
reached, assuming the centre has been expanded sufficiently, when
only a small number of people would be left on the periphery and they
would be a group with special characteristics requiring special help
and/or treatment.

Applied to education such a model, whether applied politically or
simply deployed analytically, assumes that the centre of society can
expand. More schools can be built; more courses can be made available; teaching methods can be improved; schools can be reformed and
more children can participate in an expanding structure of opportun-

ities. Halsey (1972) has referred to such assumptions as being essentially 'liberal' in character and of having been the guiding principles of educational change in the 1960s. From a research point of view this broad perspective leads to attempts to discover why it is groups on the periphery cannot participate in the expanding centre and, as is now widely known, the answers to this question involve rather complex considerations of the conditions of successful learning.

It is against this broad theoretical orientation that studies of language differences among children of different social class groups became so significant (Bernstein, 1971). Studies of language problems focused on a phenomenon which, in a sense, summarised a whole series of subtle variables which affect the capacity of different children to benefit from schooling. Language use, arguably, gives the essential clue to such factors as family attitudes and socialisation patterns (Brandis and Henderson, 1970) and, more generally, to the cultural values a family underwrites (Stubbs, 1976). And since, in any case, language is the vehicle of comprehension and communication it seems in some way obvious that linguistic factors, with their complex social roots, are implicated in the differential attainments of schoolchildren. Indeed, it is the obviousness of such arguments which explains their ready acceptance by educators, a group of people who experience such group differences in learning in a direct way in the course of their work and who are now, in my opinion, the most articulate 'carriers' of the view that class differences in attainment are a product of class specific patterns of socialisation. The results of the vast amount of research which has been conducted on this and related themes have been discussed recently by Tyler (1977) and Robinson (1976).

The political, as opposed to the theoretical, assumptions of much of this work include, at a minimum, the following. Firstly, it is assumed that the greater educational participation of particularly working-class children, which could follow from more opportunities being made available, would result in a whole group of people improving their marketable skills and therefore their life chances. In this way, formerly disadvantaged groups could be brought into the expanding centre of society and society would be changed in the direction of greater equality of opportunity. Those who could not respond to new opportunities could be specially helped to overcome their handicaps by special programmes specifically directed at them or the areas in which they live. This line of argument is made very explicit by the research on educational priority areas which followed from the Plowden Report of 1967 (Central Advisory Council for Education, 1967; Halsey, 1972).

A second assumption was that, particularly with respect to children on the periphery, the educational system could be sufficiently flexible to identify groups of children at risk and respond to their needs and discriminate positively in their favour in such a way that such children could move into the centre. Finally, although by no means exhaustively, it was and is assumed that such developments are possible without fundamental changes in education itself or in the way in which education is financed, managed and ultimately controlled.

The experience of the past ten years, however, throws into question the validity of these assumptions of this whole centre–periphery approach to educational inequality. It is now clear that education is a blunt instrument of social engineering which only works as an instrument of change under very special conditions. These conditions are those of economic growth and political consensus about the desirability of change in education. Up until the early 1970s both conditions existed although the political fissures over issues such as comprehensive schools and public spending on education were beginning to widen. And during the sixties there was indeed a rapid expansion in educational participation. More children than ever before stayed at school; more children than ever before took various school examinations. On a casual inspection of the evidence it would have to be concluded that the centre had expanded significantly. Table I indicates something of the growth in education during this period.

TABLE I
School leavers by examination attainment

Qualifications	Percentage gaining qualifications			
	1964–65	1969–70	1974–75	1979–80 (Projected)
2 or more 'A' levels	10	12	12	13
5 or more 'O' levels	8	8	8	9
No qualifications	65	47	22	—

Source: 10th Report from the Public Expenditure Committee, *The Attainments of the School Leaver*, Vol. 2, p. 9, H.M.SO. 1977.

What is not so clear, however, is whether this gowth represents a substantial increase in opportunities or indicates a shift in our society to greater educational equality. Certainly, changes in various measures of educational participation occur slowly and are likely to remain slow.

TABLE II
Pupils as a percentage of the age-group staying at school for years shown

Age	1961	1966	1972	1975	1980	1985
16	21·5	27·7	35·9	50·8	53·0	55·7
17	11·7	14·8	20·7	20·2	22·1	24·3
18+	4·1	5·1	7·2	6·7	7·8	9·0

Source: adapted from *Social Trends, 1976,* Table 3.5, p. 88, H.M.S.O. 1977.

Table II illustrates this point with data predicting the relative proportions of each age group who will stay on at school up to 1985. Given the known correlation between staying on at school and acquiring school qualifications (Department of Education and Science, 1977) it seems clear that the number of children who will acquire such qualifications will remain quite stable. Nor is it clear what such qualifications actually mean in labour market terms. Professor Dore (1976) has suggested that all over the world a process of 'qualification inflation' has set in as a result of which the qualifications required of particular types of jobs are escalating thereby reducing the value of educational certificates. The recent report of the Public Expenditure Committee (1977) drew attention to this worrying process. And a recent Organisation for Economic Cooperation and Development report (1977) concluded a review of educational credentialism in the following way:

> That some depreciation in the value of most educational qualifications has occurred in most O.E.C.D. countries is certain. It is equally certain, however paradoxical this may appear, that educational qualifications are increasingly being used by large firms and the public sector as a basic screening device when new employees are being recruited to all but the most unskilled jobs. It is also well established that for many occupations the basic educational qualifications needed has been rising steadily. This has resulted in unrealised expectations for many school and college leavers at all levels, although the position of young people with very few or no qualifications is the most acute. (p 92)

It may be the case, therefore, that what appears as the expansion of opportunities to more children is in reality something much less than that in real terms. The position of different groups of children in the labour market may have changed very little indeed. From the point of view of equality there is even less reason to be sanguine. Granting a marked improvement in the overall numbers of children who leave school with some form of educational certificate, there is still a clear social class gradient of academic success as Table III indicates. Children from non-manual social backgrounds are much more likely to gain high academic qualifications than children from manual social backgrounds. We have to conclude, therefore, that the simple expansion of opportunities is not in itself sufficient to bring about real changes to a fairer society or to change the centre–periphery relationship.

TABLE III
Academic attainment of pupils shown against occupation of father: percentage of sample gaining G.C.E.s and C.S.E.s

| | | Occupation of father | |
		non-manual	manual
	High	34	11
Academic			
attainment	Medium	34	32
	Low	32	57

High: 5 G.C.E.s or C.S.E.s grade 1.
Medium: 1–4 G.C.E.s or C.S.E.s.
Low: 0 G.C.E.s or C.S.E.s.

Source: adapted from *Social Trends, 1976*, H.M.S.O. 1977.

The conclusion should not be drawn from this, however, that further expansion of education is not a desirable end to seek or that further change in the state system of education along the road to a truly comprehensive system of secondary schooling is also undesirable. In fact, there is no firm conclusion to be drawn at all. What must be done instead is to consider the way in which questions about education and equality have been posed. In our 1971 paper (Byrne and Williamson, 1971) we suggested that: "Too much emphasis on the socio-cultural factors which are taken to influence educational attainment can divert attention from the educational system itself, its institutionalised policies and the structure of its operation" (p 6). At that point in time we were very concerned to show that inequalities in the distribution of school resources among local education authorities were still unjustifiably

large and that such material inequalities had a direct bearing on patterns of school attainment. The debate over this question has been a
heated, inconclusive one and the twists and turns in the argument have
been simply set out by John Eggleston (1977). For my present purposes
it is only necessary to take note of the fact that resource and provision
inequalities among local authorities, within local authorities and within
schools are still great and that the system of financing education
through local taxation, central government grants and the rate support
grant does not in any way afford real opportunities for reducing these
inequalities. Indeed, it has been argued recently in a case study of
education financing in a period of inflation and public expenditure cuts
that this system actually reinforces already unjustifiable inequalities
among schools (Bird, 1977).

What is also a little clearer now is that theoretical assumptions about
the social conditions of learning which were, and still are, so ten-
aciously held by teachers and politicians alike, and which David Byrne
and I did not examine in detail, are themselves highly contentious. The
work of Labov (1969) and Dittmar (1976) on language has attempted
to show that working-class children do not, in fact, suffer from a linguistic handicap and that to claim that they do is to fall into the trap of
believing that standard English or English based on the so-called 'elab-
orated code' is the only form of English speech or writing which is
precise, grammatical and capable of sustaining complex thoughts and
sequences of argument. Labov has tried to demonstrate that, from a
purely linguistic point of view, these assumptions are false. And
Dittmar has tried to show that, not only are they false but they perform
a pernicious social function of bolstering up the *status quo* by seeking to
assimilate working-class children into a dominant culture, of which a
particular attitude to and use of language is the most subtle defining
characteristic. Such theories perform this function to the extent that
they are believed in by teachers, planners and politicians but, even
more perniciously, by working-class people themselves who come to
think of their own skills and cultural capacities as being in some way
inferior. And Ginsburg (1972) has, in a similar vein, criticised some
prevailing notions of intelligence. Quite apart from some scientific difficulties with the concept of intelligence—Ginsburg feels, for instance,
that intelligence is wrongly conceived of as a 'unitary mental ability'
which some children have in greater proportion to others when, in fact,
the notion of intelligence covers a much more complex range of cognitive and creative processes—there are severe practical problems of
intelligence testing which ought to make all those who use such tests
extremely cautious. He argues in this respect that test performance

reflects the conditions under which tests are taken and also the motivation of children to succeed at such tests. On both practical counts he argues intelligence tests cannot measure the competence of lower-class children. If this is true then the use of test results to explore more complex questions of the genetic transmission of intelligence is a fundamentally flawed scientific endeavour.

It is not sufficient to question the explanatory power of various sociocultural accounts of educational inequality; the structure and operation of schools themselves must be examined, too. Subsequent work by David Byrne and myself led us to conclude that historical charters of schools, whether they were designed to be grammar schools or secondary modern schools, reflect themselves in the level of resources made available to the school in the form of buildings and facilities and in the range of examinable courses the school can offer. In our study of secondary schools in one northern local authority—Sunderland—we noted a clear connection between the provision of courses and the number of children taking them (Williamson and Byrne 1977). This observation is consistent with the findings of John Eggleston (1974) and his study of rates of staying on at schools in the Midlands. What he found was that when examinable courses are offered children tend to stay on at school to take them and this variable provision explains more fully the differences in rates of staying at school than do social-class variables describing the backgrounds of children. The conclusion I would wish to draw from such studies, although tentative, is that what schools offer has an important bearing on what they achieve; the more schools can offer, therefore, in terms of courses and the effective guarantees they can make that pupils will succeed in these courses, the more they will be able to produce children who, in a conventional sense, are successful at school.

It is not clear at all what the mechanism is which lies behind this process. Apart from the obvious mechanisms of resource distribution which distinguish schools from one another there is some evidence that there is something in the climate and organisation of schools themselves which, irrespective of the background of the pupils entering them, affects levels of performance among children. Reynolds, Jones and St. Leger (1976) concluded a preliminary review of the evidence from a study of inter-school differences in a homogeneous working class area with the observation that:

> In our opinion, and even on the basis of our analysis so far, the belief that a school can only be as good or as bad as the character and ability of the children entering it, is simply wrong. It has had wholly adverse con-

sequences for the teaching profession. We believe that teachers and head teachers have everywhere been encouraged to reduce their efforts to help the underachieving child by the growth of this climate of opinion. Children are not necessarily born to fail. What goes on in school between nine and five *is* an important determinant of the type of child that emerges at the end of the process. (p. 225)

In a study of the differences among nine schools they were not able to account for the differences they observed in attendance rates, delinquency and entrance into the local technical college—the latter being a real measure of success in this locality—on the basis of social background differences among children themselves. The differences had, therefore, to be attributed to school variables themselves although what these are the authors do not say.

Paradoxically, while no-one can identify precisely what it is which would make up the good high-achieving school there is a sufficient body of literature and research now available to alert us to practices and attitudes which might inhibit some children at school and particularly working-class children. As Pierre Bourdieu (1974) has argued, schools function subtly to reproduce social hierarchies by transforming them into academic ones. Some of the mechanisms in this process include early streaming, the so-called 'expectancy effect' whereby teachers' expectations directly influence pupil performance, biasing in the curriculum so that pupils considered to be less academic are not given access to academic courses and, of course, preselection policies for schools themselves. In addition, the attempt which schools make to impose on some children a set of beliefs and values which are inconsistent with those of the home or the community creates a great gulf between pupils and effective learning and between parents and schools themselves.

The point I wish to make is that many of these processes and variables can be controlled. The argument that educational changes towards a more just society are unlikely to be successful should be made after the point when schools have been made more equal and when the pedagogic practices of schools are purged of their self-fulfilling consequences on social selection in education. Until such conditions have been achieved then it is both dangerous and unsound to claim that change in education can have little effect in reducing social inequalities. Unfortunately, however, the likelihood is that the variables which we could control will be manipulated the wrong way. There is little political support in the 1970s for radically egalitarian policies in education. Perhaps even more worrying, the social and economic conditions which would reinforce the inequalities in the educational system itself—bad housing, youth unemployment, public expenditure cuts—are likely to persist into the foreseeable future. When such factors are combined with a professional reluctance among teachers to rid themselves of the categories of social classification as these infuse their professional assessments of children then the outlook for change in schools must appear bleak.

The centre of modern British society, just to extend the metaphor, can thus be shown to be deeply implicated in multiplying the inequalities which its own expansion is designed to eradicate. This underlines the argument which I have already made that whether educational change can make some contribution to a more equal society depends upon the circumstances in which that change takes place. Education is a blunt instrument of change but it need not necessarily be an ineffective one.

In the present circumstances, at least in Britain, the most realistic radical programme for education is one which tries to ensure that the inequalities of the centre are resisted in the schools themselves and that those parts of the system which can be controlled, and particularly the way in which resources are allocated among schools, are controlled in such a way that unjustifiable inequalities among social groups are not exacerbated.

It may be that there are limits to how far different groups in society can benefit from education which are determined by forces, either genetic or cultural, beyond the scope of education policy to control or change. There are obviously limits, as Marxist writers have been most eager to point out, to how far a truly egalitarian system of education is possible in a society whose productive base generates so much inequality (Bowles and Gintis, 1976: Dittmar, 1976). But in the absence of a system of education which is scrupulously fair and does not contain within itself mechanisms which perpetuate social inequalities then the search for those limits is absurdly premature, even scurrilous.

This was the point David Byrne and I tried to underline in 1971. Given the failure of liberal policies to achieve their ends during the sixties and early seventies, the point has still a great deal of force. For public expenditure cuts, inflation and political apathy threaten to disadvantage the disadvantaged even further and it will all be explained as if those who lose out have only themselves to blame. New situations require a new politics but they also force us to think again about how we understand theoretically the subtle links between education and society. The conditions of the late seventies invite questions about the nature of the centre, not of the periphery.

References

Bernstein, B. (Editor) (1971). *Class Codes and Control*, Vol. 1. *Theoretical Studies towards a Sociology of Language*. London: Routledge and Kegan Paul.

Bird, C. (1977). *Gateshead: A Study of Educational Inequality*. North East Area Study Working Paper No. 43. University of Durham.

Boudon, R. (1973). *Education, Opportunity and Social Inequality: Changing Prospects in Western Society*. New York: John Wiley.

Bourdieu, P. (1974). The school as a conservative force: scholastic and cultural inequalities. In *Contemporary Research in the Sociology of Education*, edited by J. Eggleston. London: Methuen.

Bowles, S. and Gintis, H. (1976). *Schooling in Capitalist America*. London: Routledge & Kegan Paul.

Brandis, W. and Henderson, D. (1970). *Social Class, Language and Communication*. London: Routledge & Kegan Paul.

Byrne, D. S. and Williamson, W. (1971). *The Myth of the Restricted Code*. Working Paper No. 1. Department of Sociology and Social Administration, University of Durham.

Byrne, D. S., Williamson, W. and Fletcher, B. G. (1975). *The Poverty of Education: A Study in the Politics of Opportunity*. London: Martin Robertson.

Central Advisory Council for Education (1967). *Children and Their Primary Schools*. The Plowden Report. London: HMSO.

Department of Education and Science (1977). Evidence submitted to the Public Expenditure Committee (1977). In *The Attainment of the School Leaver*. London: HMSO.

Dittmar, N. (1976). *Sociolinguistics*. London: Arnold.

Dore, R. (1976). *The Diploma Disease*. London: George Allen & Unwin.

Eggleston, J. (1974). Some environmental correlates of extended secondary education in England. In *Contemporary Research in the Sociology of Education*, edited by J. Eggleston. London: Methuen.

Eggleston, J. (1977). *The Ecology of the School*. London: Methuen.

Ginsburg, H. (1972). *The Myth of the Deprived Child*. Englewood Cliffs, N.J.: Prentice-Hall.

Gouldner, A. (1964). Metaphysical pathos and the theory of bureaucracy. In *A Reader in Complex Organisations*, edited by A. Etzion. New York: John Wiley.

Halsey, A. H. (1972). *Educational Priority, EPA Problems and Policies*. London: HMSO.

Jencks, C. *et al.* (1973). *Inequality: A Reassessment of the Effect of Family and Schooling in America*. London: Allen Lane.

Labov, W. (1969). The logic of non-standard English. In *Tinker, Tailor, The Myth of Cultural Deprivation*, edited by N. Keddie. London: Penguin.

Organisation for Economic Co-operation and Development (1977). *Selection and Certification in Education and Employment*. Paris: OECD.

Public Expenditure Committee (1977). *The Attainments of the School Leaver*, Vol. 2. London: HMSO.

Reynolds, D., Jones, D. and St. Leger, S. (1976). Schools do make a difference. *New Society*, July 29.

Robinson, P. (1976). *Education and Poverty*. London: Methuen.

Stubbs, M. (1976). *Language, Schools and Classrooms*. London: Methuen.

Tyler, W. (1977). *The Sociology of Educational Inequality*. London: Methuen.

Williamson, W. and Byrne, D. S. (1977). The structure of educational provision and patterns of educational attainment: A local authority case study. In *Urban Education 3*, edited by P. Raggatt and Merrill Evans. The Open University, Milton Keynes.

The Effectiveness of Schooling—Some Recent Findings from the National Child Development Study

KEN FOGELMAN

National Children's Bureau, London, England

Over the last decade or so one can trace an increasing lack of confidence in the importance of schools as determinants of children's educational progress. Major reports such as Wiseman (1964), the work of Douglas and his colleagues on the National Survey of Health and Development (Douglas, 1964; Douglas *et al.*, 1968) and the early reports from the National Child Development Study (Davie *et al.*, 1972), have consistently shown how great is the relationship between children's attainment and such factors in their family background as their fathers' occupational group, their family size and their parents' interest in their schooling.

By contrast school variables have been shown to have only a slight relationship, if any at all, with their pupils' attainment. Even the International Study of Mathematics Achievement (Husen, 1967), comparing entire systems of education, failed to provide clear evidence of any marked, consistent relationships. Perhaps most influential of all has been the much publicised American contribution to this debate, most notably by Coleman and others (1966) and the more recent work of Jencks and his colleagues (1973). Together these and other studies have led to an air of pessimism, such as that shown by one reviewer when concluding that they 'cast doubt on any belief that increased inputs in education automatically mean better quality output' (Woodhall, 1972).

My purpose in this paper is to attempt to ensure that this evidence is not misinterpreted, and to support my own interpretation with some recent findings from the National Child Development Study. I am not suggesting that the various authors mentioned above have not interpreted their findings correctly, but I certainly do believe that others have taken them too far, and in particular when they have been introduced into the domain of public discussion they have led, for example, to the use of such slogans as 'Does School Really Matter?'— and not always couched in this interrogative form.

The crucial point to note is that studies such as those referred to above are able only to relate *variation* among schools to *variation* among pupils' attainment. While one can therefore correctly conclude that there is little relationship, if any, between children's attainment and such variables as school size, class size, pupil–teacher ratio, teacher turnover, ability-grouping, parent–teacher contact etc., one must limit one's conclusions, firstly to the context of *existing* variation among schools—changes beyond the range of values in the above variables reasonably common in schools as they now are might bring about a quite different pattern—and secondly to the context of variation and not go beyond this to dismissing schooling *per se* as being unimportant.

It is in relation to this second point that I wish to present some of our recent findings, but before doing so I should like to define our understanding of the relationship between attainment and social variables of the kind mentioned in the first paragraph above. As this, and all the other results which I shall be presenting, arise from the work of the National Child Development Study (NCDS), it is necessary first to give a brief description of that study.

The NCDS has its origins in the 1958 Perinatal Mortality Survey carried out by the National Birthday Trust Fund. For this study, all the babies born in the week 3–9 March 1958, throughout England, Scotland and Wales received a special examination at the time of their birth and mothers were interviewed shortly afterwards, providing details of the pregnancy and some aspects of social background, for the main purpose of identifying factors associated with stillbirth, early mortality and handicapping conditions (Butler and Alberman, 1969).

The NCDS came into being in 1964 when the National Children's Bureau received a grant to carry out a follow-up of these 16,000 or so children in the following year when they were aged seven. The scope of the study was widened to examine educational and social as well as medical development, and the first report from the study was published as an appendix to the Plowden Report. A comprehensive account of the seven-year stage of the study was published in 1972 (Davie *et al.*, 1972).

Subsequent follow-ups have been mounted in 1969, when the children were aged eleven (Davie, 1973) and 1974, at the age of sixteen (Fogelman, 1976). The methods of data collection at each of the three stages have been essentially similar, involving a medical examination by local authority medical officers, an interview of the parent (by health visitors) and the completion of a questionnaire and the administration of tests by the schools. At eleven there was a small, and at sixteen substantial, questionnaire completed by the children themselves.

Perhaps the above gives some indication of the quantity of data which the National Children's Bureau now holds on these young people and it is clear that in the time available, this paper can only hope to give some flavour of the work that has been done. To date twelve books and some 150 papers have been published and anyone interested in other aspects of our work can obtain a list of these publications from the Bureau.

For the past four years the study has been funded by the Department of Education and Science and the Department of Health and Social Security to enable it both to continue to analyse the data collected at birth, seven and eleven and to carry out the third follow-up, and then to carry out further analyses incorporating the sixteen-year data. The analyses described in this paper represent just a small sample of the work carried out in that period.

Firstly, then, the importance of family background variables for children's attainment: as already mentioned the relationship between educational attainment and, for example, social class and family size has been well documented in a number of studies. A further question of theoretical importance and practical relevance is whether such differences are stable. For example, do the differences between children of different social class, known to exist when they first enter school, remain approximately constant throughout their schooling, or does the gap between the social classes increase, or decrease.

Figure 1 presents NCDS data relevant to exactly this question, by showing for each social class the average reading test score at eleven for children with a given reading test score at seven. It can be seen that, apart from the lowest scores where numbers are rather small, the three lines are clearly distinct, demonstrating that for children of equal attainment at seven, those with fathers in non-manual occupations have, by eleven, moved ahead of those with fathers in manual occupations. Between seven and eleven there is an increasing gap between children of different social classes. Taking the extreme comparison, and making a very approximate conversion to age-equivalents, those in the non-manual social classes have moved a further 1·4 years ahead of those in social class V, additional to the pre-existing difference at seven of 1·6 years.

A similar pattern is found in relation to family size.

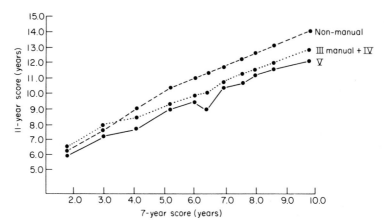

FIG. 1. Social factors associated with changes in educational attainment between 7 and 11 years—reading scores and social class.

Figure 2 presents the data in the same way for mathematics attainment and different family sizes. Again it can be seen that in general those children in small families have by the age of eleven moved yet further ahead of those in larger families. (A detailed description of this work can be found in Fogelman and Goldstein, 1976.)

Given then the overwhelming importance of such factors, what can be done by our schools? Can they hope to play any part in influencing children's development, in reducing inequalities which are apparently so largely socially determined? Even teachers, one often feels, have been

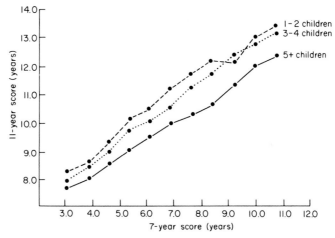

FIG. 2. Social factors associated with changes in educational attainment between 7 and 11 years—mathematics scores and family size.

influenced by such findings to the extent that they expect very little from children from disadvantaged backgrounds, and willingly hold social background responsible for a child's failure—although they may be more ready to take credit for success.

That schools do play a more important role than this attitude implies can I think be shown by three examples drawn from quite different aspects of recent NCDS work. In introducing these may I stress that they are recent, as yet unpublished and in one case at least require further analysis, but the findings are sufficiently firmly-based to illustrate my point.

The first example concerns age of starting school. England and Wales are rare among European countries in not having a single school-starting date for each year group, and it is now over a decade since the Plowden Committee suggested that this might be changed. There is considerable evidence for the simple relationship between length of schooling and subsequent attainment. On the other hand it has not been clear that this relationship is due to the amount of time spent in school as such. Autumn-born children are more likely to enter infants' school at an earlier date in the school year. That these children do subsequently show higher average attainment may be due to the greater time they have been in school, but several alternative explanations have been offered, such as the effect of being the youngest in a class, with teaching levels appropriate to average children; or the younger child's problems in joining an already established class; or the effect of teachers' expectations, which may be higher for older children.

The NCDS data are in fact well-suited to an attempt to resolve this question since, on the one hand all the children in the study are of the same age and, on the other hand, once those with formal pre-school experience are excluded (and this was comparatively rare in 1963 when they were starting school), they divide approximately equally into those who started school before their fifth birthday and those who started later (i.e. with typically one term's difference in the length of schooling).

Of course it is still not enough simply to make the straightforward comparison between these two groups—the 'early' and 'late' starters. There are other difference between them which could account for subsequent differences in attainment. For example, the 'early' starters are slightly more likely to be middle-class and there are considerable regional variations in the age of starting school.

Table I summarises the results of an analysis of variance which takes into account a large number of such background variables. The 'unadjusted' figures represent the simple difference between the mean test

TABLE I

Age of starting school and attainment at eleven

Differences in eleven-year test scores (in months):
early starters minus late starters.

	Unadjusted	Adjusted*
General ability	4·9	2·6
Reading	4·4	2·3
Mathematics	4·3	2·6

* After adjusting for the following factors: social class, family size, region, sex, parental education, teacher's rating of parental interest in child's progress, tenure of home, crowding, class size, attendance rate.

scores of the two groups and the 'adjusted' figures are the results of allowing for all the listed factors, that is essentially comparing children whose characteristics are similar for each of the variables named. As can be seen this reduces the contrasts by about half, but there still remains a statistically significant difference between the two groups.

My second example relates to school attendance. On the face of it, it may seem obvious that children whose attendance rate is poor do less well at school. Whether this is a cause and effect relationship, and if so in which direction it works, is more problematic, but at least one would predict fairly confidently that such a relationship exists. However, what evidence there is on this suggests that this prediction is by no means as straightforward as might have been expected.

Douglas and Ross (1965), for example, related composite scores on reading, vocabulary, intelligence and arithmetic tests taken at the age of eleven, to attendance records over the preceding four years. Although in general they did find a relationship between average scores and attendance, this did not hold for their 'upper middle class' group, among whom even those who had averaged about eight weeks' absence per year obtained test scores no lower on average than the best attenders.

Analysis of NCDS data at the age of eleven produced a similar result (Fogelman and Richardson, 1974) with the relationship between attendance level in that year and reading, arithmetic and general ability tests reaching statistical significance only for children whose fathers were in manual occupation.

Figure 3 summarises part of a rather fuller analysis which we have recently been able to carry out using the sixteen-year data for the same children. This shows the association between attendance rate (in the Autumn term, 1973) and mathematics test scores from an analysis of variance which also took into account attendance rate at the age of seven, sex, region and housing circumstances as represented by an index of overcrowding. As can be seen there was a significant interaction in the findings, that is the relationship was not the same for each social class, but this is mainly due to the group of children with no male

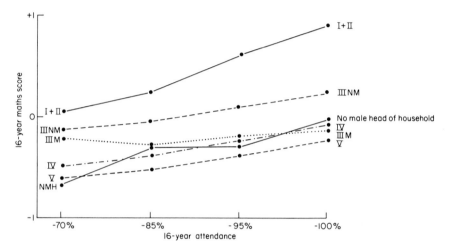

Fig. 3. 16-year mathematics score: attendance at 16 × social class interaction.

head of household, and for the other social classes the relationship is reasonably clear, although somewhat flat for the skilled-manual group. In a similar analysis of reading test scores the pattern of results is even more straightforward with regular increments in the average reading test score for each attendance level and for each social class.

My third and final example is taken from the work of three colleagues (Richardson, Ghodsian and Gorbach, in preparation) who have been examining, *inter alia*, the relationship between mathematics test scores at sixteen and the number of hours per week spent on mathematics lessons. This analysis is at the preliminary stage in that it presents only the straightforward relationship (but for different kinds of secondary school) and we have seen above how this can sometimes change when relevant backgrounds are taken into account.

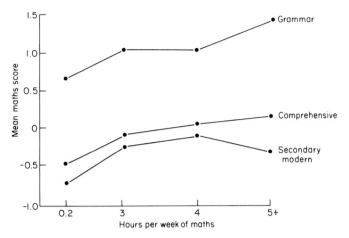

Fɪɢ. 4. Hours per week of maths lessons and mean maths scores at 16.

Figure 4 shows, on the whole, a steady increase in mathematics test scores according to the number of hours spent on mathematics (children in remedial classes, who might have artificially depressed the scores of those spending most time on mathematics, are excluded from the analysis). The notable exception is among those in secondary modern schools where those with five or more hours per week of mathematics lessons obtained slightly lower mean scores than those with three or four hours of lessons.

We have seen within all the findings which I have presented some such slight departures from the overall pattern, but in general these findings amount to a demonstration that children's attainment is related to the quantity of schooling which they have received.

Of course these analyses are, as well as being preliminary, correlational and it would be wrong to deduce cause and effect directly from them. However they are consistent in their direction in three quite separate contexts, and they certainly show more marked relationships than have been found in those analyses which measure the importance of schooling through administrative variables such as those mentioned earlier. While it remains true that we do not know how, if at all, we might affect children's development by changing such features of schools as their size or type or pupil–teacher ratio, the results I have been presenting here should serve as an antidote to those who wish to write off the educational enterprise altogether on the grounds that children's attainment is solely the function of variables drawn from outside the school system.

References

Butler, N. R. and Alberman, E. D. (1969). *Perinatal Problems*. Second Report of the British Perinatal Mortality Survey. Edinburgh: Churchill Livingstone.

Coleman, J. S. *et al.* (1966). *Equality of Educational Opportunity*. Washington, D.C.: U.S. Government Printing Office.

Davie, R. (1973). The second follow-up of the National Child Development Study. *Statistical News*, **22**, 14–18.

Davie, R., Butler, N. and Goldstein, H. (1972). *From Birth to Seven*. London: Longman, in association with the National Children's Bureau.

Douglas, J. W. B. (1964). *The Home and the School*. London: MacGibbon & Kee.

Douglas, J. W. B. and Ross, J. M. (1965). The effects of absence on primary school performance. *British Journal of Educational Psychology*, **35**, 28.

Douglas, J. W. B., Ross, J. M. and Simpson, H. R. (1968). *All Our Future*. London: Peter Davies.

Fogelman, K. (Editor) (1976). *Britain's Sixteen-Year-Olds*. London: National Children's Bureau.

Fogelman, K. and Goldstein, H. (1976). Social factors associated with changes in educational attainment between 7 and 11 years of age. *Educational Studies*, **2**, 2.

Fogelman, K. and Richardson, K. (1974). School attendance: some results from the National Child Development Study. In *Truancy*, edited by B. Turner. London: Ward Lock.

Husen, T. (1967). *International Study of Achievement in Mathematics: A Comparison of Twelve Countries*. New York: John Wiley.

Jencks, C. *et al.* (1973). *Inequality: A Reassessment of the Effect of Family and Schooling in America*. New York and London: Basic Books and Allen Lane.

Richardson, K., Ghodsian, M. and Gorbach, P. (in preparation). The association between school variables and attainments in a national sample of sixteen-year-olds.

Wiseman, S. (1964). *Education and Environment*. Manchester: Manchester University Press.

Woodhall, M. (1972). *Economic Aspects of Education*. Slough: National Foundation of Educational Research.

The Galton Lecture 1977:
Educating Girls—'To Repair the
Ruins of Our First Parents'

MARGARET B. SUTHERLAND

School of Education, University of Leeds, Leeds, England

The title of this lecture partly derives from a statement of aim made by John Milton (1644) in his *Tractate of Education*. This borrowing does not mean that I am going to advocate a scheme of education of which Milton would necessarily have approved, for in Milton's view we could repair the ruins of our first parents only by regaining to know God aright and when he turned to a second or secular aim, preparation for "all the offices both private and public of peace and war" he had boys rather than girls in mind. But the title seemed appropriate to indicate both the need to improve the state of society to something nearer to the Garden of Eden and the need to improve the education which not only the first but many generations of parents and others have given to girls. My theme is in fact that by changing the traditional approach to girls' education we may benefit by a greater contribution from women to the general well-being of society; a better education of girls leading to social betterment.

The quotation has also the merit of recalling an enduring concept of the role of woman, as exemplified in the myth of those first parents; for, according to that myth, woman can be seen as having a primary responsibility for the loss of paradise and therefore, along with responsibility to try to repair that initial error, some degree of guilt for the non-paradisical state in which the world has been for many centuries. Or, taking a contemporary interpretation of the myth, we might say that on the primal occasion woman showed divergent thinking and a strong drive to explore the unknown, even when this meant opposing divine authority; the results of this behaviour were so cataclysmic that, by a kind of aversive conditioning, the descendants of Eve have since that time respected all authority as divine, carefully obeyed the rules and refrained from exploring beyond the prescribed way.

Certainly, whatever the influence of the traditional interpretation of the myth, our society has for long accepted that the contribution of most, if not all, females to the well-being of society lies in satisfactory performance of the role of wife and mother. Proposals to improve society by educating girls to play this role more effectively can be traced in many writings on education. Nearly two hundred years ago, for example, Pestalozzi, concerned for the improvement of life in the villages of his native land, suggested in *Leonard and Gertrude* (1781) that the wise and diligent mother could educate her children in the home and so raise the standards of life not only of her own family but of the whole community. This view of woman's contribution to social betterment flourished throughout the nineteenth century; it motivated various voluntary or charitable organisations to provide for the education of women so that the lot of the poor could be improved. When the Medical Department of the Board of Education became responsible for the physical well-being of children in schools, Dr Newman (1911) emphasised that teaching Infant Care to girls was highly important: "The schools . . . afford the best practical means of training the working-class mother to take care of her child." Today we find statements that in underdeveloped countries the education of females must not be neglected since to educate a woman is to educate not an individual but her whole family. One can see the apparent advantages of this model of education. A society composed of families who have each a good mother who is thrifty, skilled in effective household management, knowledgeable about health and diet, even contributing aesthetic adornments to the home, cannot fail to be a good and happy society. The model has also the advantage of providing girls with a clear aim in life and a clear role definition. It has undoubtedly brought to society many benefits and given many women a highly satisfying and happy life. Admittedly, it has also caused much dissatisfaction: and it does seem often to have meant entering into a career of domestic worker for which there are no trade unions, no controlled conditions of work, no set salary scales, no agreed holidays with pay, no prospects of promotion, no pension scheme but eventually a fair prospect of redundancy. (In view of these factors, the success and enjoyment found in such a career by many women prove the admirable flexibility of females and their perceptive judgement of the weakness of explicit regulations and the advantages of fringe benefits.)

Yet there is obviously a need for greater improvement in society; and whatever their contribution through private life, the participation of women in public affairs has by no means been as great of that of men. Change seems to be called for. There are also factors in contemporary society which mean that the model of marriage and parenthood is changing; consequently the role of wife and mother is differently defined and requires, possibly, new qualities. What factors of change are particularly to be noted? I shall refer briefly to four: (i) attitude to work outside the home; (ii) control of child-bearing; (iii) divorce, attitudes to marriage; (iv) public participation in decision-making.

(i) Attitude to Work outside the Home

It has of course long been known that a large proportion of the female population, whether married or not, work outside the home, in either full-time or part-time employment; though this fact has often been overlooked in discussions of women's education. But what is now noteworthy is the fact that girls are showing awareness of the probability of continuing to work outside the home after marriage. Thus, while a recent survey of fifth form girls (Rauta and Hunt, 1975) found considerable interest in marriage and children—"only 3 per cent said they definitely or probably would not marry" and "over three-fifths of the sample said that they definitely wanted children"—yet "only 9 per cent of the sample were looking forward to giving work up altogether after marriage or after having children". This acceptance of a dual role carries implications both for vocational training and for cultivation of the ability to participate in the affairs of industry and commerce.

(ii) Control of Child-bearing

Although marriage remains highly popular and although many women marry while still very young, the pattern of child-bearing has changed drastically. There is some evidence (Pearce, 1975) to suggest a pattern of postponement of the first child; and there is the overwhelming evidence of the general fall in the birthrate, e.g. the birth total for 1976 being 74·8 per cent of that for 1971 (Office of Population Censuses and Surveys, 1977). As has been noted elsewhere in this Symposium, the development of reliable contraceptive methods and their greater accessibility have been of immense importance in changing the lives of women. Such developments call for increased judgement and ability in making vital decisions.

(iii) Divorce; Attitudes to Marriage

Along with the popularity of marriage we must note the growing frequency of divorce; for example, in 1951 the divorce rate per thousand married women was 2·6: in 1974 it was 8·7 (Central Statistical Office, 1976). Many people are still staying married but undoubtedly divorce is now easier and the idea of divorce is more readily accepted. We may note also a trend about which it is inevitably difficult to secure evidence, the trend by which young people decide to live together without the formalities of marriage; such 'trial marriages' may be of varying durations—some may end in formal marriage, others in separation. One has the impression that this trend is growing stronger, at least in some social groups. In all, it does seem that marriage nowadays is less likely to be regarded as permanent. It is less obviously a 'solution' which will settle the whole future life of the woman and dictate all her future work and actions. There is thus less encouragement to girls to do as many have tended to do and leave their options open, avoiding commitment to study or career, because after all, they may marry and that will render career decisions and ambitions irrelevant.

(iv) Public Participation in Decision-making

As has been pointed out in other discussions, one of the trends in contemporary society is to involve people more frequently in public decision-making, either at community level or at national level. In education, there is increasing emphasis on consultation with parents and on their participation in the lives of schools. Thus the mother must be knowledgeable not simply about her own children but about the wider issues of education and about the political and social factors which are involved in education and in such community participation.

In these circumstances what characteristics seem to be required in women and what characteristics should their education try to develop? What would seem to be required is the ability to make important decisions reasonably, to make them with self-confidence, and to be ready to face the consequences of these decisions; to be self-reliant; to be able to cope composedly with the demands of a variety of circumstances and roles; to be concerned about the issues not only of the immediate domestic sphere but also those of society at large. Has education produced these characteristics in girls?

I am now going to consider the emotional characteristics of girls which seem to have been fostered by our system of education (in school and out of school). I consider *emotional* characteristics not because I underrate the importance of knowledge and skills; I am by no means unsympathetic to those who are at present urging that girls be encouraged to apply themselves to the study of mathematics, science and applied sciences. I agree that we should have many more women engineers and I am delighted to hear politicians say this. But it is on the affective side that our educational system is weakest; it is there that we must make modifications if we are to make good some of the errors of past generations of parents and teachers; and if we do not improve on the emotional side, modifying attitudes, then we shall not be successful either in gaining more girls for the study of science or engineering.

But let me first make a reservation which has probably already occurred to you. Differences between boys and girls, males and females, whether we are talking about cognitive skills and knowledge or about emotions and attitudes, are not absolute; our measurements of such characteristics show considerable overlap. Factors of intelligence and social class are often more important than the sex difference and differences within a sex group are often larger than differences between the sex groups. So although I am focusing on girls' characteristics, I am not suggesting that all girls are the same or that boys do not have these feelings and attitudes. I am simply considering characteristics in which, on the average, girls seem to differ from boys.

In outlining some of the emotional characteristics which seem to be found to a greater extent in girls, I am not, however, going to make the same assumption as that made by the illustrious thinker for whom this lecture is named. Fascinated, as people so often were in the later part of the nineteenth century, by the doctrine of evolution and natural selection, Francis Galton thought that some hesitation in the female's acceptance of a mate would be necessary to efficient natural selection; and thus in his *Inquiries into Human Faculty* (1883) he wrote as follows: "One notable peculiarity in the character of the woman is that she is capricious and coy, and has less straightforwardness than the man . . . Coyness and caprice have . . . become a heritage of the sex, together with a cohort of allied weaknesses and petty deceits, that men have come to think venial and even amiable in women, but which they would not tolerate among themselves." It is indeed remarkable how attitudes have changed since then—I wish that I could foresee the changes in the conceptual framework I now use which will have occurred ninety-four years from now.

Although there are a number of possible sex differences in emotional characteristics which might be discussed, I shall focus on three areas: (*a*) negative feelings (low aspirations—in career, salaries, authority; negative self-image; anxiety; dependence on external factors); (*b*) religious interests; (*c*) interest in human relationships.

(a) Negative Feelings

The first area, that of lower levels of aspirations in girls, has been so thoroughly explored that I need not illustrate it largely. Many workers have found that the vocational expectations expressed by girls are lower than those expressed by boys; for example a survey of sixth-formers' opinions (Hutchings and Clowsley, 1970) found that girls had lower expectations as to occupations, salaries and the amount of authority they would have. The tendency for girls to opt for what is considered the academically less demanding course by entering Colleges of Education rather than universities is well known; e.g. McPherson *et al.* (1972) found that Scottish schoolgirls opting for college rather than university had a relatively low self-concept of academic ability. One might suggest that the lower vocational expectations were due to interest in marriage prospects. But deprecation of their own academic performance can be found in girls well before adolescence; thus, Barker Lunn (1972), studying a group of some 2000 children in the third and fourth years of junior schools, found that "girls had a poorer academic self-image, they were more anxious in the classroom" and this despite the fact that "girls at the primary school level make faster progress and attain a higher level of achievement". Similar self-depreciation, at a later stage, is noted by Maccoby and Jacklin (1975), commenting on results of studies in the USA: "College men are more likely than college women to expect to do well and to judge their own performance favourably once they have finished their work."

Anxiety was mentioned by Barker Lunn. It is frequently found that when tests of anxiety are applied, females score higher than males. Thus Maccoby and Jacklin, reviewing some 20 researches, noted that on some (7 of the 20) no sex difference was found but "where there is a difference the girls score higher". The classic study by Sarason and associates (1960) on primary school children's anxieties found girls scoring higher than boys on both general and task anxiety tests. Possibly allied to this are the higher female scores on neuroticism scales, e.g. on Eysenck's much-used Personality Inventory. (I should here make it clear that I am not considering clinical tests of anxiety states but simply the more general group test results; but some evidence of sex differences in mental illness was given in Dr Roberts' (1976) paper to the twelfth annual symposium of the Eugenics Society.)

A further variation of negative self-feeling is lack of confidence in one's ability to control events. Evidence on this point is not clear-cut but Maccoby and Jacklin (1975) report that "in college there is a trend for women to be externalisers. That is, they believe their achievements are often due to factors other than their own skill and hard work."

For these characteristics a variety of explanations can be suggested. Most obviously, an explanation might be looked for in biological factors. Physiological changes associated with menstruation and pregnancy, for example, might explain some fluctuations of mood and uncertainty about ability to control events. Yet since differences appear before puberty it would seem that this could not be a total explanation and that causation must be, to some extent at least, social rather than biological.

On the social side, we must recognise that the legal position of women in the past has indeed meant that they could not control many important aspects of their lives; but this is, largely, now past; though young Asian women in this country may still have the decision about their marriage made by others (as may some young Asian men). There is also evidence to suggest that success by girls can be regarded as unbecoming; Horner (1970), for example, found success stories relating to girls evoking less approval than those relating to boys; and there is considerable folklore about girls trying deliberately not to outshine boys. Some study (Rapoport, 1974) has even shown that female students overestimate the extent to which males expect them to be concerned with personal rather than academic success.

As to anxiety, it has been found (e.g. Davie *et al.*, 1972) that girls are, from early childhood, more likely than boys to seek adult approval— boys tending to be more interested in peer group approval. Possibly adult approval is less predictable and less easy to ensure than the approval of the peer group? (It would be somewhat biased to suggest that, looking at a world in which the decisions of major importance— nuclear defence, unemployment rates etc.—are taken almost exclusively by men, any rational being would feel anxious.)

In general, it is not clear what exactly is the origin of the negative feelings in question; but it does seem clear that at least to some extent social conditions can affect and encourage them; hence education has to be concerned about them.

(b) Religious Interests

Both sexes receive the same religious teaching within the public educational system (though in confessional schools the religious atmosphere within boys' and girls' schools may show more differences). Yet it is commonly found, in this country and elsewhere, that girls express more interest in religious studies. Thus the Schools Council Enquiry

Young School Leavers (1968) found that a considerably greater proportion of girls than boys rated religious studies as interesting and useful. For the adult level, Argyle and Beit-Hallahmi (1975) in the *Social Psychology of Religion* review a number of surveys and a number of criteria of religious behaviour and conclude that: "It is obvious that women are more religious on every criterion." (It is interesting to note that these authors suggest, *inter alia,* the greater occurrence of guilt feelings among females as an explanation for this stronger attachment to religion.)

Now this characteristic can have both advantages and disadvantages. On the negative side, although religion properly understood should not develop feelings of sex inferiority or superiority, the churches' hierarchy at present gives an impression of male dominance since priests, ministers, religious leaders are, by an overwhelming majority, men (and indeed the Russian Orthodox Church has recently affirmed the need for exclusively male ministry). Psychoanalytically, this factor could be interpreted as adding to the attraction of religion for women; but other interpretations are possible. In non-Christian religions too one can find factors encouraging a submissive attitude and feelings of inferiority in females. One notes that even the language of Christianity, in English, tends to emphasise the dominance of the male by its references to God the Father and God the Son; a woman achieves honour as the Mother of God, which has clear role-definition implications. Yet changes in this aspect seem improbable—the suffragette exhortation: "Pray to God, my dear, and She will help you!" inevitably continues to sound incongruous.

Yet other aspects of religion have clearly positive values. Religious teaching does emphasise the development of a self-concept and the critical measurement of the self against clearly stated standards of what is right and wrong. Satisfying these standards—or attempting to—becomes a matter of importance and reassurance; and whatever may be said philosophically about the separation of morals from religion (I am not asserting a necessary connection of the two) it remains true that in the past—and for some people, in the present—morals and religion are closely linked. It is therefore important to look carefully at present changes in the teaching of religious studies in schools and the place of such studies in the curriculum. I strongly sympathise with the wish to get rid of the very bad teaching of religion which has taken place in some schools; and it is iniquitous that teachers should be compelled to teach beliefs they do not hold to children who do not want to receive them (and legal safeguards of teachers' and children's and parents' rights do not always prevent such undesirable situations). But we must be careful that changes do not dispense altogether with an interest which has had special appeal for girls; and that new teaching adequately develops the self-concept and the awareness of standards of right and wrong which religious teaching at its best has provided.

(c) Interest in Human Relationships

The third characteristic, that of interest in human relationship, may well be linked to the religious interest. Certainly there is a great deal of popular support for the view that girls and women are more interested in personal relationships than are boys and men. Cross-culturally, one finds that women are given the nurturant role in society, the task of looking after people, caring for the children and the old especially. As we have earlier noted, women tend to assume that they do differ from men in such interest in personal relationships; and in making some of the career choices already noted, girls commonly say that they prefer the kind of job where they will be working with people/children. It is less clear whether this interest is accompanied by greater perceptiveness where the feelings of others are concerned. Sandven (1975) studying senior secondary school pupils and students in training as teachers found, using a projective test, that females did score rather higher on empathy or 'co-reaction'; but the differences between the sexes were not great. Surveys of some other researches do not show a significant sex difference in ability to interpret the feelings of others; indeed Maccoby and Jacklin (1975) suggest that: "the social judgment skills of men and boys have been seriously underrated." What is remarkable, given the socially acceptable interest shown by females in the well-being of others, is that this interest has not been developed to include interest in social and political affairs. Many studies have shown that girls and women are less well-informed than boys and men about such matters; and they tend to vote less. The recent study of *The Political Awareness of the School Leaver* (Stradling, 1977) found that "boys are indeed more politically knowledgeable than girls". Yet the Schools Council *Enquiry* (1968) showed, if anything, rather greater interest among girls than among boys in the study of history (at the 15-year old stage), and subjectively I have the impression (confirmed by some discussions with educators in other countries) that girls more than boys show interest in associations fostering international understanding; and girls' schools—and girls in coeducational schools—have been active in community service. But again the international study of *Civic Education in Ten Countries* (Torney et al., 1975) found that in the great majority of cases boys made higher scores and showed more interest than girls in civic education. Indeed, as the researchers remarked in some astonish-ment, as a subject of the curriculum civic education seemed to come into the same category as maths and science where a distinct sex differ-ence showed greater success and involvement on the part of boys.

Such circumstances indicate a discrepancy between the interest girls show in human relationships and the development of that interest for social involvement. Too often, one suspects, the interest is allowed to dissipate itself in the reading of fiction; we have evidence (Schools Council, 1975) that in adolescence girls read more than boys but boys read more non-fiction than girls. At school, is the choice of fiction studied helpful or simply encouraging to day-dreaming? Even Jane Austen's works may leave the impression that the happy *ending* for the female is marriage to an eligible man. In general, the interest shown by girls in human relationships, while strong in the immediate situation, does not seem to be extended by education to social and political events.

From this rapid survey then it appears that the educational system today sends into society girls who, on the average, tend to have a negative evaluation of themselves so far as achievement and career are concerned, are anxious, not certain of their control over events, not greatly interested in the decisions and organisations which affect society in general. However compatible these characteristics may be with con-tributing to social well-being through the role of wife and mother, they are not really compatible with the circumstances of the present day, with the changing concepts of marriage and family life and with the improvement of social conditions.

Change therefore is needed in educating the emotions of girls, both within schools and outside schools. An indication that such change would be acceptable by girls themselves can be found in another of the results of the Schools Council *Enquiry* (1968). Pupils were invited to indicate the relative importance of a number of possible objectives for schools, including such things as the development of personality and character, being able to deal with people and be at ease, becoming able to stand on one's own feet, becoming aware of differences between right and wrong. "All of these items concerned with self-development were markedly more generally held to be highly desirable objectives of their school course by girls than by boys."

How, then, do we educate emotions? Not, in my view, by the intro-duction of new subjects, intended solely for emotional development or by exotic stimulation of emotions. Admirable as some experiences of drama, miming, role-playing may be we are not yet certain exactly what is achieved by the emotional behaviour encouraged in some such situations.

It is not enough to stimulate emotions and hope that this will be a beneficial effect. We need to know what emotions are being encouraged—and this is by no means easy to assess—and our purpose is not simple stimulation but education. At another extreme, possibly, behaviour modification techniques do not at present give an answer to our problem. They may well be useful for small manageable items of behaviour in which emotional reinforcement can be given or withheld in a clearly recognisable situation; but as yet we have not sufficient knowledge or control of circumstances to apply such techniques to major aspects of emotions.

What then can be done in the educational system? (I do assume that education can have an effect on society, despite various problems in the way of achieving an effect.) There are three kinds of changes in schools which might contribute substantially to improvement of the kind hoped for. These changes would be in the structure of school life, in the content of books and other materials used in teaching in schools and in the development of imaginative and rational discussion of roles in society and in politics.

(1) Changes in the Structure of School Life

We hope, of course, that the general atmosphere of schools will be such as to produce feelings of pleasure and achievement in their work. But there are ways in which the organisation of schools and of their extra-curricular activities can subtly convey information about sex-typing and can encourage boys and girls to feel that they must conform to the expected norms for their sex. It is encouraging to know that in 1975 two reports by Her Majesty's Inspectors drew attention to some such influences—the report on *Curricular Differences for Boys and Girls* (Department of Education and Science, 1975) based on a survey of English schools, and the report on *Differences of Provision for Boys and Girls in Scottish Secondary Schools* (Scottish Education Department, 1975). These reports show how choices of subjects and vocational preparation can be affected by the type of school—coeducational or single-sex—and the attitudes in the school towards subject choices. Perhaps most surprisingly, it was realised that coeducation does not necessarily lessen sex differences in attitudes towards subjects; it may even increase them. And other evidence (Elliott, 1973) indicates that in discussions within the coeducational school, boys and girls may be responding to different pressures; though the discussion is open, girls may feel it their place to keep quiet and let the boys talk. Now that such evidence is becoming more widely known, the staff of schools who are aware of such influences will be able to modify their methods to counteract them where necessary; they will be able to consider whether, for example, the kind of activity expected of boys and girls on special occasions—speech days, official visits to the school etc.—is going to confirm traditional sex-typing by giving girls the function of serving tea or coffee while boys engage in public speaking. If girls are to be self-reliant and participate actively in public life, they must have practice. It is more difficult to know how schools can counteract the influence of the staff hierarchy since, as the Scottish Report pointed out, in coeducational schools it is highly probable that more men than women will occupy the senior posts.

(2) Analysis of the Content of School Books and Other Materials

Just as the influences guiding boys and girls towards sex-stereotyped choices of subjects have been recognised of late, so too have the implications of some of the school texts been recognised. It has been pointed out that from the early stages of education school books do tend to present men and women in 'traditional' roles—the reading book shows mummy staying at home while daddy goes out to work and so on. History books occasionally tend to give the impression that for centuries the population consisted entirely of men—no activities by women are recorded, except for an occasional inept performance by a woman trying to rule. Even audio-visual courses in foreign languages may work hard to gain the sympathy of the learners by reinforcing heartily the popular stereotypes of girls' gossip and boys' interests. The topic of sex education itself can lend itself to such bias; for example, a handbook recently published to help parents and teachers with sex education (White and Kidd, 1976) proposes the following comments in discussion with boys: "Marriage implies a high calling for a man—as a husband, as a father and as the head of a family . . . men should think out what qualities a girl looks for in a man to share her life with, and usually, the more feminine and the more attractive girls do look for a boy who will be protective and decisive . . . in a word masculine." Realism, though also some subtle conditioning, creeps in with the corresponding comment for girls: "A husband needs to be stable and reliable, and you've got to live with him not only when he's looking his best, but when he's got a cold in the nose or a boil on his neck, and sits sleepily taking no interest in you across the breakfast table."

If therefore we are aware of the effect of the expectations conveyed by teachers' attitudes in the everyday circumstances of the school and the effect of aspects of school books which are not central to the teaching process—but none the less powerful—it should be possible to make the necessary changes; provided that we have clearly in mind the emotional qualities which we want to produce, the feelings of self-reliance and freedom from anxiety.

(3) Imaginative and Rational Discussion

More positively, if we hope to educate emotions, even with our limited knowledge and limited techniques, what we must do is to attempt the integration of emotion and reason. If emotion is to be helpful, it must be in response to situations which are perceived clearly and understood well. We must therefore provide more opportunity to discuss reasonably and imaginatively matters of importance in human relationships of daily life and of importance in the policies of society. In such discussions both girls and boys can begin to understand more clearly the factors which are important in dealing with other individuals and in dealing with groups of individuals. I stress that such discussion must be imaginative. It is not enough to engage in abstract reasoning; the people who are discussing must be able to feel for those involved in the situation under consideration. This, as I have indicated elsewhere (Sutherland, 1971), is the contribution of imagining and the best use to which that ability can be put. And here the techniques of drama, the use of television and films, visits and role-playing, may very well be appropriate to bring to the discussion those emotional responses which will give realism to the situation and point to the rational discussion. And among the subjects for such discussion should be the roles of women and men in society today. This is, as I have noted, by no means an easy part of education; but it is one which is most likely to have enduring results, if only we can find the teachers to use such an approach as it should be used. It is helpful to note that some education in the discussion of topics of social importance has been provided in Sweden for some time (Marklund, 1977); the results, so far as they can be judged, showing some successes though also some problems, especially with regard to teacher qualifications. Of course, it may be that social influences outside the school remain stronger than those inside the school. It is also possible that girls might, in spite of the school's endeavours, choose to continue to avoid involvement with the wider society, to remain playing a subordinate role leaving decision-making to others. If that is their choice, then they must be allowed to make it; but they should make the choice in fuller awareness of the circumstances and with the ability to choose freely.

By this time it is probably clear that in talking of this change in education I am not dealing with education suitable only for girls. For both sexes the avoidance of unthinking sex-stereotyping is important; for both it is important not to be subtly edged into vocational and other decisions simply because of traditions about what suits one sex or the other. For both it is important to be knowledgeable, clear-thinking and sympathetic in dealing with social problems. Some differences in methods may be necessary to deal with tendencies in which the sexes differ; but the ultimate purpose of such education is the same and the reorganisation of school life and materials should be for the benefit of both sexes. Thus in trying to improve the education of girls, we also improve that of boys; and, as we noted earlier, there is in fact much that they have in common in emotions, attitudes and interests.

If the educational system can make the changes proposed we may not only free girls from some of the erroneous assumptions which have led them to envisage their contribution to society as restricted to the limits of the family but we may help to develop in all members of society what Francis Galton (1883) indicated as desirable for the further evolution of the human race "the new mental attitude . . . of a greater sense of moral freedom, responsibility, and opportunity." Then without constraint both sexes may take pleasure in the fruit of the tree of knowledge and society, the human race itself, may at last enjoy the fruit of the tree of life.

References

Argyle, M. and Beit-Hallahmi, B. (1975). *The Social Psychology of Religion*. London: Routledge and Kegan Paul.

Central Statistical Office (1976). *Social Trends*, No. 7. London: HMSO.

Davie, R., Butler, N. and Goldstein, H. (1972). *From Birth to Seven*. London: Longman, in association with the National Children's Bureau.

Department of Education and Science (1975). *Curricular Differences for Boys and Girls*. London: HMSO.

Elliott, J. (1973). *Sex Role Constraints on Freedom of Discussion: A Neglected Reality of the Classroom*. Norwich: Centre for Applied Research in Education, University of East Anglia.

Galton, F. (1883). *Inquiries into Human Faculty and its Development*. London: Macmillan.

Horner, M. S. (1970). Femininity and successful achievement: basic inconsistency. In *Feminine Personality and Conflict*, edited by J. M. Bardwick, E. Douvan, M. S. Horner and D. Gutman. Belmont, California: Brooks Cole.

Hutchings, D. and Clowsley, J. (1970). Why do girls settle for less? *Further Education*, **2**, 6–7.

Lunn, J. C. B. (1972). The influence of sex, achievement and social class on junior school children's attitudes. *British Journal of Educational Psychology*, **42**, 70–74.

Maccoby, E. G. and Jacklin, C. N. (1975). *The Psychology of Sex Differences*. London: Oxford University Press.

McPherson, A., Flett, U. and Jones, C. (1972). *After Highers Project*. Research Paper No. 1. Department of Sociology, University of Edinburgh.
Marklund, S. (1977). *Civic Education in Swedish Schools since 1945*. Stockholm: National Board of Education.
Milton, J. (1644). *Tractate of Education*. Edited by E. E. Morris (1911). London: Macmillan.
Newman, G. (1911). Report of the Chief Medical Officer. Cited in Morality and the medical department: 1907–1974, by P. W. Musgrave (1977). *British Journal of Educational Studies*, **XXV**, 142.
Office of Population Censuses and Surveys (1977). *Population Trends*. London: HMSO.
Pearce, D. (1975). Births and family formation patterns. *Population Trends*, **1**, 6–8. London: HMSO.
Pestalozzi, H. (1781). *Leonard and Gertrude*. Translated by E. Channing (1901). Boston: D. C. Heath.
Rapoport, R. N. (1974). Sex differences in career development at three stages in the life cycle. *SSRC Newsletter*, **24**, 7–10.
Rauta, I. and Hunt, A. (1975). *Fifth Form Girls: Their Hopes for the Future*. London: HMSO.
Roberts, D. F. (1976). Sex differences in disease and mortality. In *Equalities and Inequalities in Health*, edited by C. O. Carter and J. Peel. London: Academic Press.
Sandven, J. (1975). *Projectometry*. Oslo: Universitetsforlaget.
Sarason, S. B. *et al.*, (1960). *Anxiety in Elementary School Children*. New York and London: John Wiley.
Schools Council (1968). Enquiry 1, *Young School Leavers*. London: HMSO.
Schools Council (1975). *Children's Reading Interests*. London: Evans/Methuen Educational.
Scottish Education Department (1975). *Differences of Provision for Boys and Girls in Scottish Secondary Schools*. Edinburgh: HMSO.
Stradling, R. (1977). *The Political Awareness of the School Leaver*. London: The Hansard Society.
Sutherland, M. B. (1971). *Everyday Imagining and Education*. London: Routledge and Kegan Paul.
Torney, J. V., Oppenheim, A. N. and Farnen, R. F. (1975). *Civic Education in Ten Countries*. London: John Wiley.
White, M. and Kidd, J. (1976). *Sound Sex Education*. London: Order of Christian Unity.

How Preventive is Medicine?

P. E. BROWN

Department of Community Medicine
University of Sheffield, Sheffield, England

How preventive is medicine? Obviously this is not a question that requires a formal answer. I shall take it, therefore, as an invitation to discuss the place of medicine in social repair, insofar as this is assumed to be ideally preventive.

The basic relationships between medicine, disease and social breakdown are twofold (Philip, 1908; Segerstedt, 1962). First, illness impairs the individual's ability to cope with his social environment; and medicine by curing or preventing disease can prevent social breakdown. Second, faults in the social environment are among the causes of disease. Correction of social faults, therefore, can prevent illness and promote health.

Recent interest in the second of these relationships, the social causes of disease, has popularised the idea that medicine is a social science and that the physician, especially the general practitioner, is a social worker in the community (Senault, 1961) whose primary role is to prevent disease by controlling those factors in the individual's personal and family life which lead to a breakdown of the normal working of his body or mind (Barber, 1951). The field of work of the general practitioner, it has been said, has no formal limit (Gillie Report, 1963).

In consequence, many people, including the Labour Party in its evidence to the Royal Commission on the National Health Service (*The Times*, 1977) believe that the country's resources should be diverted away from the supposedly narrow hospital-based clinical medicine and given instead to prevention and primary care. Clinical medicine is thought of as old-fashioned. Preventive medicine, especially a preventive medicine allied to the behavioural sciences, is regarded as the new concept and the medicine of the future.

How do these ideas stand up to examination against the background of medical and social history?

Preventive medicine is far from being an exciting new development. It is as old as Hippocrates and has always occupied a respected place in medical literature. This is all the more remarkable when we remember that for most of the time its methods have been completely useless. That is to say scientifically useless; but not socially useless. The scientific purpose of preventive medicine is to control the incidence of disease. Its social purpose is to allay anxiety by giving the public a confident feeling that there is some barrier between them and sickness and death.

For this it does not need scientific methods. Anything will do as long as people believe in it and since, all in all, more people remain well than become ill a reputation for effectiveness by even an inert remedy is not difficult to acquire. The only thing is that, for its reputation to last, a remedy's mode of action must be compatible with prevailing ideas on the causation of disease.

Whiting and Child (1953), in a cross-cultural study, came to the conclusion that it was the prevailing ideas on the causation of disease rather than the physiological utility of the prophylactic measures themselves which decided whether people believe in, say, dietetic methods, cleanliness, regulation of bowel action, regulation of sexual habits, prayer, protective isolation or disinfection and the killing of germs. These ideas the authors related to child-rearing practices and their associated anxieties, oral, anal and sexual, and anxieties over dependency and aggression. Caudil (1953), thinking along the same lines and drawing on the experience of an American team working with cholera in China, suggested that it was easier to introduce new therapies if you did not try to change people's ideas at the same time. He quoted Dr Hsu, a Chinese-American, as saying that while science had to be disguised as magic in China, in America magic had to be dressed up as science.

The medical man in a pre-scientific society is the personification of the inert remedy, giving reassurance and relief from anxiety and taking the blame when things go wrong. To cope with his problems he has had to invent a system of ingenious devices many of which have been passed down and institutionalised in modern medicine. To retain the respect of the patient he cannot cure he asks: "Why didn't you call me in sooner?" To the patient who gets better of his own accord he can say: "Its a good job you got me when you did". This does not mean, as Bernard Shaw said, that professions are conspiracies against the laity or as Kafka (1920) wrote in one of his letters "doctors are stupid, or rather, they are not more stupid than other people but their pretentions are ridiculous." The conspiracy is *between* the doctor and the layman.

The layman *has* to preserve his faith in doctors, in success stories, and the marvels of modern medicine. The doctor's pretentions are a reluctant adaptation to the ridiculous expectations and demands of society.

But doctors have always had enough science to deal with bleeding and broken bones; and bit by bit they have added to their knowledge so that nowadays they do not have the same need to practice the *art* rather than the *science* of medicine. But even medical science has its pitfalls and the history of the conquest of scurvy illustrates some of the difficulties in answering the question: *how preventive is medicine?*

Scurvy had always been endemic in northern Europe and North America. It became widespread in the sixteenth century when the invention of the mariners' compass made possible long sea voyages without fresh food. The sailors soon found out from the Scandinavian farmers, the American Indians and people in other places they visited that fresh vegetables, infusions of pine needles and citrous fruits were valuable cures and prophylactics. In 1605, Captain James Lancaster, of the East India Company, took bottled lemon juice for his men on a voyage round the Cape (Roddis, 1951; Davidson and Passmore, 1969). Bacon's *New Atlantis*, in 1627, mentioned the benefits of oranges. In the next century, Captain James Cook kept his ships supplied with fresh foods and vegetables. On land at about the same time scurvy became rare after the potato replaced other crops in the course of the agricultural revolution (Hirsch, 1885; Salaman, 1949). But the cause of the disease was not established until 1928, when Szent Gyorgi, a biochemist working on reducing substances in animal tissues, happened to discover ascorbic acid which was later identified with the hitherto hypothetical Vitamin C.

What was the medical contribution to this success? As I have described it, very little indeed. The doctors merely wrote down in their books what they had learned from the farmers, the sailors and the Red Indians. In 1747, the Scottish Naval surgeon, James Lind, to satisfy his own curiosity about what was already known, gave twelve sailors with scurvy six different treatments and observed that the two who got lemons and oranges made a remarkable recovery (Lind, 1752). Does this make the conquest of scurvy a medical discovery? Yet Lind's experiment, among a number of similarly unsubstantiated success stories of the past, is quoted as an example of the way in which the modern *epidemiological method* has made, and by implication will continue to make, crucial contributions to our knowledge of the causation of disease (Morris, 1957; Brown, 1961, 1964).

What does all this amount to? It means that the problems inherent in the question *how preventive is medicine* are these: where do we draw the

line of demarkation between the medical and the non-medical contribution to the prevention of disease? To what extent is this line of demarkation blurred by the inflated claims made on behalf of preventive
medicine to meet the pretensions of doctors and the expectations,
demands and anxieties of the public?

As a further illustration I shall now examine some of the progress
made in disease control by the Victorians, their immediate predecessors
and their contemporaries in other countries. This brings me to Johann
Peter Frank. Johann Peter Frank was a German physician who became
in 1785 Professor of Clinical Medicine in the University of Pavia and in
the following year Director-General of Public Health for the province
of Austrian Lombardy. As a clinician with an interest in the well-being
of the population he wrote two papers: '*The misery of the people is the
mother of diseases*' and '*The civil administrator is the most successful physician*'.
Frank taught that the way to health was the abolition of poverty by
good government (Sigerist, 1956).

This doctrine was resented both by the medical profession as an
invasion of their rights and by educated laymen who were unhappy at
the prospect of a redistribution of wealth. In Scotland, however, it was
taken up by two physicians, Professor Cowan of Glasgow and Professor
Allison of Edinburgh who kept on insisting that the root causes of
epidemic disease were poverty and destitution (Ferguson, 1948). Later
on, in 1901, Rowntree (1901) showed that the wages of the average
worker in York were insufficient to supply the physiological necessities
of life. Ewart (1923) pointed out that the otherwise unexplained decline in tuberculosis was closely correlated to a rise in real wages and
many writers since have confirmed the effects on mortality and morbidity of economic factors which affect the general standard of living.

What we can say, therefore, is that left to themselves and given the
resources, ordinary people will intuitively choose a healthy way of life.
And we can also say: social progress, quite as much as medicine, is
responsible for modern improvements in health; and, thirdly, laymen
have no need for professional help in doing what they can perfectly well
do for themselves.

But the Victorians were unimpressed either by Johann Peter Frank
or by the Scottish physicians. They looked to Edwin Chadwick, the man
with the 'sanitary idea'. Chadwick was the architect of the Poor Law
Amendment Act of 1834 and one of the commissioners appointed to
implement its provisions. His approach was pragmatic. Poverty was a
burden on the poor rate and on society. This burden was augmented
by the high rates of sickness among the poor. Their sickness was due to
the squalor in which they lived. For Chadwick the link was not be-

tween poverty and disease but between dirt and disease. He began, therefore, to improve sewerage, refuse disposal and water supplies—not for drinking but for washing. This appealed to the Victorians. Whereas Johann Peter Frank wanted to promote health by getting rid of poverty, Chadwick wanted to reduce the burden of sickness by keeping the poor clean and without disturbing the existing social order.

Chadwick's English Sanitary Movement became the model for public sanitary services throughout the world. But sanitary science, although it prevents disease is not preventive medicine. Sanitation specialists are not doctors. They are for the most part environmental health officers, and sanitary and water engineers.

What, then, is left of preventive medicine when we take away sanitary technology as well as non-medical social progress? There is bacteriology, immunology, nutritional science and industrial hygiene. But again, specialists in these subjects are not specialists in preventive medicine. They are often not doctors.

So when people talk of diverting resources from hospital or clinical medicine to preventive medicine, what do they mean? To which of these diverse preventive activities do they propose to allocate their funds? Can they say that money spent specifically on preventive medicine will prevent disease whereas money spent elsewhere in medicine, or biology or technology will not? Preventive medicine on its own can do little more than monitor health statistics and administer and co-ordinate the work of other specialties. These are its *scientific* functions. But its *social* function is to maintain a reassuring presence as a barrier between the public and death and disease. It can do this by keeping up a flow of success stories based on legendary achievements of the past and unfulfilled promises for the future—the epidemiological jam of yesterday and tomorrow.

Turning from preventive medicine itself to the preventive role of primary medical care we must again go back to the Victorians. It was their social and scientific progress which not only increased our control over disease but also determined the attitudes, anxieties, expectations and demands of modern society. In the nineteenth century there were two dominant influences—religious and scientific. The religious influence is typified by Charles Kingsley's *Sanitary Essays* (Kingsley, 1880) in which the ten commandments were supplemented by laws of health, and freedom from disease was regarded as the reward for obedience to these laws. As a result the promotion of health became a kind of religious duty and prophylactics such as vaccination became divine gifts whose efficacy and safety no right-thinking person was entitled to question. The Victorian religious influence is still discernible in the evangelical and uncritical fervour with which some of our contemporaries attack the problem of health and prevention.

The scientific influence, on the other hand, generated a public demand for modern scientific medicine. Every scientific discovery in the early years of the century had to have its unscientific place in medical practice. Faradism, galvanism, magnetism, the new gases, the microscopic fungi, each produced a crop of the most bizarre therapeutic and aetiological theories. In the search for the cause of cholera, for example, people systematically measured the electrical potential of the atmosphere or went up in balloons with butterfly nets to catch the microscopic fungi they thought would become visible as they swelled up with the reduction of barometric pressure. In the later years and into the present century things became more restrained but the sciences multiplied and diversified and doctors acquired the habit of combing through the new branches of physics, chemistry, biology, psychology, sociology and even computer technology in the hope of finding answers to their intractable professional problems. In their turn the scientists began to look to medicine for opportunities for their own particular disciplines and the combined process has now been made respectable under the heading *Widening the horizons of medicine*.

The Victorians, however, with their narrower horizons were less receptive than we are to the antics of those they regarded as dunces and imposters. Their concern was the use being made of more down-to-earth discoveries. Sir Robert Philip, speaking in 1906 of Koch and the tubercle bacillus said:

> Twenty-five years have well-nigh passed since the essential cause of consumption was definitely determined and announced to the world . . . Yet, this evening, the question forces itself urgently, what practical benefit has accrued therefrom to the communities of men? Have *communities* enjoyed the fruits to which they are entitled from Koch's great epoch-making discovery? (Philip, 1906)

His answer was: "No", and twelve years later Lord Dawson of Penn again called for the benefits of medical knowledge to be brought within reach of the people (Dawson, 1918). In 1920, Sir George Newman of the Ministry of Health declared: "A different kind of doctor is needed in these times" with an improved training in new subjects – preventive medicine and "the political science of communal responsibility" (Newman, 1920). In 1924, the *Lancet* presented the case for a future general practitioner who was to be easily accessible to his patients, competent to deal with the beginnings of disease and able to advise on health matters and preventive measures.

But the ground was already beginning to shift. Lloyd George's National Insurance Act of 1911 had taken the first step towards government control of medical practice. On re-reading Newman's paper it then becomes clear that his plea for an improved training in "the political science of communal responsibility" is an elegant way of saying that: if society is to interfere with the doctors, the doctors had better learn to interfere with society. Medicine no longer adapts itself to the demands and expectations of society, it begins to adapt society to the demands and expectations of medicine.

A second feature of Lloyd George's scheme was the capitation system whereby doctors were paid an annual fee for every insured person on their list. It was intended as no more than a convenient way of dividing funds among the doctors in amounts roughly proportional to the work done. As things turned out, it gave a new meaning to the word *patient*. The patient was not just someone who went to the doctor when he was ill. He was someone on the doctor's list all the time, whether he was sick or well. This was not the original intention of the scheme. The capitation system was adopted merely because the Stationery Office could not produce the forms needed for the method of payment originally suggested (Braithwaite, 1957). But the effect was to establish a new principle: that "the medical service of the community must be based on the provision for every individual of a general practitioner or family doctor." (*British Medical Journal*, 1930.) The doctor then had an obligation to the healthy person as well as the sick person on his list. He could discharge his obligation to the sick by medical treatment. The only thing he could do for the healthy was prevent. So the horizons of medicine had to widen. The general practitioner had to break away from his 'narrow clinical obsession with the diseased part' and draw on the resources of the behavioural sciences to cope with the *whole person* who had nothing very much wrong with him. He had to become the family doctor who, according to the *British Medical Journal* of 1930, was to be a trusted *regular* adviser, a guardian of the health interests of the family, a repository of the confidence of members of the family, the director of the family on health matters, the adviser on preventive measures.

Is this what the public really wanted? The public in 1930 was already beginning to short-circuit general practitioners and go straight to specialists. This tendency was deplored by the British Medical Association (*British Medical Journal*, 1930) as "foolish, uneconomic, bad for the patient and bad for the medical profession". "The public must recognise," they said, "as the medical profession does, that the family doctor is the foundation of any complete and efficient medical service."

Did the preventive role of the family doctor arise out of the need to bring new scientific knowledge within reach of the public? Again the evidence suggests not. What was the scientific knowledge on prevention available to the general practitioner which he, rather than the medical officer of health, was in a position to bring within reach of the public? Going by the standard medical textbooks of the period it amounted to this: moderation in all things; avoid whatever upsets you.

Has nothing been learned since about the relationships between psycho-social factors and the breakdown of the normal working of body and mind? Certainly there is a wealth of statements about *the* relationship between *the* social environment and *disease*. But we are sadly lacking in particular instances of *a* relationship between *a specific* social variable and *a specific* disease.

No topic has been more intensively studied than the relationship between psycho-social factors and cardiac infarct. In a three-day conference on socio-environmental stress and cardio-vascular disease held in Phoenix, Arizona in 1966, socio-cultural changes, and social, demographic, inter-personal and psychological characteristics were exhaustively discussed in papers quoting hundreds of references. All that could be said out of a mass of inconclusive or contradictory evidence was that it was "sufficient to *suggest* that social factors *may* play a *definite* role in the aetiology of coronary disease" (italics inserted) and Edward Suchman summed up with the remark that the overall impression was "one of an overwhelming epidemiological infarct" (Marks, 1967; Suchman, 1967).

It would seem, therefore, that the physiological utility of the preventive methods we can offer does not as yet come up to the demands and expectations of either the public or the profession. Our present task is not to bring new knowledge within reach of the people but to bring these demands and expectations within sight of reality.

In its quest for reassurance by prevention, modern society appears to have traversed the whole Freudian spectrum, from the anal anxieties of the sanitarians, the oral anxieties of the nutritionists, the sexual anxieties of psychotherapists, the aggression of the germ killers it has finally arrived at the dependency anxieties implicit in primary medical care. But who have the problems, the patients or the doctors? Are we perfectly sure that a caring profession is not just an interfering profession?

How preventive is medicine? What remains after this process of demarcation and deflation? The answer is: a lot more than you might think. The doctor who works as a clinician and diagnoses efficiently and treats efficiently can prevent a sizeable amount of social disrepair. Some years ago in a study of rheumatoid arthritis we found that the patients whose social position was most improved were those in whom the medical treatment had been most successful (Duthie *et al.*, 1964). A patient with multiple sclerosis once told me how grateful she was to her doctor for getting her a new flat and a welfare telephone and then added, "But I'd rather he'd given me my health."

How would she have reacted to the suggestion made in last year's Butterworth Gold Medal Essay that the College of General Practitioners has "acted as a major catalyst to new studies which explored the perspectives of traditional medicine, psychology, and the behavioural sciences in order to forge better models of the consulting process in both the diagnostic and interventive aspects"? (Stevens, 1977).

My own contention is that a sound clinical training and the provision of adequate facilities for doctors to work together as clinicians is the best contribution medicine can make to social repair. In conclusion, therefore, may I "explore one further perspective of the behavioural sciences"—Talcott Parsons' book *The Social System*. Parsons believes in the intrinsic connection between professional status and technical competence. He writes:

> High technical competence also implies specificity of function. Such intensive devotion to expertness in matters of health precludes comparable expertness in other fields. The physician is not, by virtue of his modern role, a generalised 'wise man' or sage—though there is considerable folk-lore to that effect—but a specialist whose superiority to his fellows is confined to the specific sphere of his technical training and experience. (Parsons, 1951)

References

Barber, G. O. (1951). The country doctor. *British Medical Journal*, **ii**, 439–441.

Braithwaite, W. J. (1957). *Lloyd George's Ambulance Wagon*. London: Methuen.

British Medical Journal (1930). The British Medical Association's proposals for a general medical service for the nation. Supplement, **i** (April 26), 165–182.

Brown, P. E. (1961). John Snow—the autumn loiterer. *Bulletin of the History of Medicine*, **35**, 519–528.

Brown, P. E. (1964). Another look at John Snow. *Anesthesia and Analgesia*, **43**, 646–654.

Caudil, W. (1953). Applied anthropology in medicine. In *Anthropology Today*, edited by A. L. Krowber. Chicago: University of Chicago Press.

Davidson, S. and Passmore, R. (1969). *Human Nutrition and Dietetics*. Fourth Edition. Edinburgh: Livingstone.

Dawson, B. (1918). The future of the medical profession. *British Medical Journal*, **ii**, 23–26.

Duthie, J. J. R., Brown, P. E., Truelove, L. H., Baragar, F. D. and Lawrie, A. J. (1964). Course and prognosis of rheumatoid arthritis. *Annals of the Rheumatic Diseases*, **23**, 193–204.

Ewart, R. J. (1923). Economics in tuberculosis. *Proceedings of the Royal Society of Medicine*, **xvi**, 2 (Epidemiology Section), 1–18.
Ferguson, T. (1948). *The Dawn of Scottish Social Welfare*. London: Nelson.
Gillie Report (1963). The field of work of the family doctor. *Report of the Sub-Committee of the Standing Medical Advisory Committee of the Central Health Services Council.* London: HMSO.
Hirsch, A. (1885). *Handbook of Historical and Geographical Pathology*, Vol. 2. London: New Sydenham Society.
Kafka, F. (1920). *Letters to Milena* (1953). London: Secker and Warburg.
Kingsley, C. (1880). *Sanitary and Social Essays*. London: Macmillan.
Lancet (1924). The future of health insurance. **ii**, 759–760.
Lind, J. (1752). Treatise on scurvy. Cited in *Human Nutrition and Dietetics*, edited by S. Davidson and R. Passmore (1969). Edinburgh: Livingstone.
Marks, R. (1967). A review of empirical findings. In Social Stress and Cardiovascular Disease, *Milbank Memorial Fund Quarterly*, **XLV** (No. 2, part 2), 51–108.
Morris, J. N. (1957). *Uses of Epidemiology*. Edinburgh: Livingstone.
Newman, G. (1920). The state and the future of medical practice. *British Medical Journal*, **ii**, 33–36.
Parsons, T. (1951). *The Social System*. London: Routledge & Kegan Paul.
Philip, R. W. (1906). Public aspects of the prevention of consumption. *British Medical Journal*, **ii**, 1 December. In *Collected Papers on Tuberculosis*, edited R. W. Philip (1937). London: Oxford University Press.
Philip, R. W. (1908). The anti-tuberculosis programme: co-ordination of preventive measures. Transactions of the International Congress on Tuberculosis at Washington, D.C., 21 September–12 October 1908. Reported in *Collected Papers on Tuberculosis*, edited by R. W. Philip (1937). London: Oxford University Press.
Roddis, L. H. (1951). *James Lind*. London: Heinemann.
Rowntree, B. S. (1901). *Poverty: A Study of Town Life*. London: Macmillan.
Salaman, R. N. (1949). *History and Social Influence of the Potato*. London: Cambridge University Press.
Segerstedt, T. T. (1962). Socialmedicinen och samhällsvetenskaperna. In *Socialmedicinska Skrifter*, 1. Stockholm: Svenska Bokförlaget.
Senault, R. (1961). Letter in *The Times*, 23 September. London.
Sigerist, H. E. (1956). *Landmarks in the History of Hygiene*. London: Oxford University Press.
Stevens, J. L. (1977). Quality of care in general practice: can it be assessed? Butterworth Gold Medal Essay, 1976. *Journal of the Royal College of General Practitioners*, **27**, 455–466.
Suchman, E. A. (1967). Appraisal and implications for theoretical development. In Social Stress and Cardiovascular Disease, *Milbank Memorial Fund Quarterly*, **XLV** (No. 2, part 2), 109–113.
The Times (1977). Labour proposals on NHS criticise 'narrow' doctors. 17 June. London.
Whiting, J. and Child, I. (1953). *Child Training and Personality Development: A Cross Cultural Study*. New Haven: Yale University Press.

Problems of Medical Audit

IAN McCOLL

Guy's Hospital, London, England

Over the past few years there has been increasing interest in what is generally known as medical audit, which is concerned with the evaluation of medical care. "Clinical appraisal" was proposed as an alternative to medical audit (McColl, 1976) because *audit* suggests a threat to clinical freedom or bureaucracy dictating to the profession (Thompson, 1976). The original meaning of audit was a judicial hearing of complaints; later it came to mean an official examination of accounts by independent agents. By contrast, clinical appraisal should be an educational exercise leading to improvements in patient care. However inappropriate the term medical audit may be, it is probably here to stay. In the past years there have been a number of attempts to improve the quality of medical care, all of them relying on a greater degree of objectivity than has hitherto been the case.

Confidential Enquiry into Maternal Mortality

The confidential enquiry into maternal deaths was started in 1952 and great credit should go to the obstetricians for being so far ahead in this field (Godber, 1976). It would be well to look at the reasons for the success and acceptability of this enterprise. First, confidentiality; second, the principle of looking at a system rather than checking on an individual; third, immediate relevancy to the work in hand; and, fourth, its educational rather than punitive nature.

United Kingdom National Quality Control Scheme

This scheme was started in 1969 to survey 200 pathology laboratories which carried out clinical chemistry analyses (Whitehead, 1976). Assessment has been made of performance in some of the more common investigations. Participation is voluntary and laboratories remain anonymous. The findings are presented in such a way that the participants can judge their own performance, particularly in relation to the analytic method used. An assessment of factors affecting the variance of results such as laboratory automation, analytic methods and workload has been made. Recent results suggest that reliability within and between laboratories has been improved.

Death and Complication Meetings

At Guy's Hospital we have introduced techniques of clinical appraisal which have been established in the USA and have also experimented with some of our own (McColl *et al.*, 1976). Death and complication meetings have been held weekly. The five surgical teams in turn present all their own deaths and complications. Various consultant surgeons preside over the meetings and foster a friendly atmosphere in which personal recrimination is out of place. Abrasive criticism tends to encourage doctors to wriggle out of embarrassing situations rather than learning from them, and might destroy the more sensitive person who had already learned the lesson from his mistakes weeks before the case was discussed at the meeting. The identity of the surgeon whose case is under discussion is not normally known.

This is a painless and popular method of clinical appraisal whose main emphasis is educational. It offers a weekly refresher course which is relevant to all participants. Many problems which might otherwise remain hidden are brought to light and resolved. This type of meeting is as relevant to physicians as surgeons and its widespread introduction might do much to improve standards of care.

Problem Orientated Medical Records

Problem Orientated Medical Records were adopted officially by Guy's Hospital in 1974. They have many advantages over conventional records. Because they promote better communication it is easier to maintain continuity of care—a matter of increasing importance with the complexity of modern medicine and the reduction in working hours of the junior staff. As we have gained experience with the Problem Orientated Medical Records, their educational function has become clear. They provide a means of reviewing the logic of the management plans of all members of the firm. Inappropriate plans are immediately apparent and can be corrected. Problem Orientated Medical Records help students learn to make rational management decisions by encouraging them to record their observations and conclusions in a prescribed manner.

Occasional Surveys

Death and Complications meetings often bring to light a complication or a clinical problem which is on the increase. A controlled clinical trial or, if such is not appropriate or acceptable, a simple prospective survey can then be initiated. For instance, two years ago the incidence of burst abdomen seemed to be increasing and a clinical survey was agreed upon. Each surgeon performing a laparotomy was asked to complete a questionnaire at the end of the operation recording all the relevant information. Within six months of the inception of the survey the incidence of burst abdomens fell tenfold. At the same time on the gynaecological firms, which were not included in the survey, the incidence of burst abdomen remained constant. If a problem is looked at carefully it may well disappear.

Review of Resources

A "review of resources" committee was born of necessity because there is an ever increasing problem of acute medical and surgical beds being blocked by chronically sick and geriatric patients who cannot be placed in more suitable accommodation without inordinate delay. To try to improve the situation, a committee to review the resources was set up to inquire into all patients who had been in hospital for more than two months. This is not a critical or punitive exercise, but simply designed to help the clinician and the patient. It has been generally welcomed. This procedure is bringing to light many constraints which exist within the system that have been an irritation to the clinicians and have never been systematically tackled before.

Unit Review Meetings

During the past year we have held weekly review meetings which are private, are attended only by medical staff and have the purpose of examining any facet of the work of the firm which is thought to be unsatisfactory in order to evolve policies acceptable to all. The focus of a session may, for example, be the use of a certain surgical technique, a decision on pre-admission investigations, a debate on how ward rounds should be conducted, or a discussion of the long-term management of a particular problem patient. In all these discussions it is not only the clinical aspects that are dealt with but also the economic implications and the administrative difficulties. We think this is important to broaden the outlook of the junior staff as to their future roles in the profession, because it is quite clear that doctors will have to accept much more responsibility for the management of available resources than has previously been the case.

We probably made an initial mistake in calling them 'audit meetings' because the junior staff were decidedly uneasy at first. This gradually gave way to acceptance, and then to enthusiasm as it was appreciated that in these meetings all men are equal.

Attempts to Measure the Quality of Care

With the setting up of problem-orientated medical records throughout Guy's the King's Fund asked us to find out whether this new system actually made a difference to patient care and so we were introduced to the problems of measurement in the field. The classical concept is that the quality of care depends on *structure, process* and *outcome*. Clearly the physical plant and organisation of an institution are important when considering the quality of care. Simply to compare the outcome in one hospital with the outcome in another may be doing an injustice to some clinicians working under antiquated conditions, with poor resources and under-staffed. The influence of structure can be described, but is difficult to measure. Process—the investigation and treatment of patients—is what clinicians are engaged in every day. Outcome—is an estimate of how well the patient has fared in the system.

The quality of care is also dependent to some extent on the patient's contribution. That is, the contribution that the patient brings to his own illness in terms of his age, obesity, previous illness, nutrition and so on. Just as one surgeon may have to contend with poor working conditions, another may be dealing with a population that is more at risk than the average. Clearly any attempt to measure the quality of care is a complicated study.

In developing our method we set certain constraints:

1. The method should be reproducible.
2. It should be applicable beyond the teaching hospital.
3. It should not be disruptive of hospital routine.
4. The data should be collected by trained clerical staff from large numbers of case notes, using explicit criteria.

The surgical cases we studied were operations for *peptic ulcer* without perforation or stenosis, *inguinal herniae* without obstruction, and *gall stones.* All the patients were more than 15 years old, and none had malignant disease. Our sources of information were Hospital Activity Analysis and the case notes. We collected the same items of information for all the diseases studied, and recorded them on mark-sense documents read directly by a computer. HAA supplied the information on age, sex, marital status, admission source, principal diagnosis and secondary diagnoses. The Office of Population Census and Surveys prepared a special breakdown of the hospital fatality ratios according to the International Classification of our disease groupings. These were substituted for the risks of age and sex. The remainder of the study data were abstracted from the case notes by four trained clerical staff supervised by the project registrar. Regular random checks were made on the clerks and their overall accuracy was excellent, with an error rate of less than 0·5 per cent. In order to make some estimate of the contribution which the patient brings to his own illness, twelve items recorded on admission were grouped together within the computer to form a patient-risk score for each case studied. Some of these were physiological measurements and others are demographic information. The higher the patient risk score, the more compromised he was at the time of admission.

In an attempt to evaluate what happened to the patient during his admission, a clinical management score was arrived at with the cooperation of a panel of clinicians at a hospital outside this study. They agreed upon a list of investigations they would consider suitable in the management of each disease, weighting each one from one to three depending on whether it was useful, desirable or mandatory for good management. A multiple regression model was used to analyse the data.

There was a positive association between clinical management score and the number of blood chemistry abnormalities, i.e. the more chemical abnormalities the patient had, the better his clinical management. The same was true of patients with peptic ulcer whose blood pressure was raised on admission, for hernia patients with hypertension or obesity and patients admitted with gall stones who had abnormalities on urinalysis. However, there was a negative association in ulcer patients between the clinical management score and the number of admissions in the previous twelve months, i.e. the more times they had been admitted in the previous twelve months the poorer their clinical management. Similarly gall-stone patients admitted as emergencies received poorer attention than those admitted as a routine. A large part of the variation in the quality of care occurred between firms, i.e. for ulcer patients 30 per cent of the variation was explained by the firm alone. When we took into account the significant risks that the patients brought to their illness it only altered that variation from 30 to 36 per cent. The same picture held true with patients with hernias and gall stones.

Clinical Information Service

As the work proceeded it became clear that there was a wealth of clinical information which was so fascinating that we felt our colleagues ought to have access to it as well. We therefore attempted to design a method of presenting this material to them in a concise way and with some explanation of the implications.

The first of these information sheets have been distributed and welcomed. They are completely confidential, hand written and there are no copies. The patients listed are identified by their hospital number and are given a numerical score according to the risks they bring to their condition. One patient for example was a female of 60 whose risk score was high because she refused to stop smoking heavily before operation, her diastolic blood pressure was 105, and she was obese. She spent one day in hospital before operation, and was discharged nine days after her cholecystectomy. The outcome column showed that she developed a chest infection and was pyrexial at the time of discharge. Even more disturbing, in the column marked 'comments', there was a note to the effect that the displaced trachea noted on routine chest X-ray was not followed up. The consultant who received this news could, of course, take comfort from the fact that it was the whole firm that was being appraised rather than him personally.

A second sheet gave information on how the firm performed over a range of basic clinical managements pertinent to the diagnoses studied. The percentage of patients who had the relevant investigations done was shown and comparisons could be drawn with the overall performance because the percentage done by all the firms together was also given. Discrepancies were immediately apparent. There is no use at all in supplying clinicians with information they do not want, and will not read. It has to be information which they agree to receive and which is easy to digest if it is to fire their enthusiasm to consider how their clinical performance can be improved.

Summary

In summary, all these methods of clinical appraisal described amount to a system which embraces these important principles. It should be:

1. An educator not a policeman.
2. Confidential.
3. Educative and interesting, providing plenty of scope for research activity.
4. Non-abrasive.
5. Non-invasive.
6. Inexpensive.

Clinical appraisal is here to stay. If we do not do it ourselves we will have it done to us.

Acknowledgements

We are most indebted to the King's Fund for a grant which has supported much of the work described in this review article, and to our consultant colleagues at Guy's Hospital for their cooperation and encouragement.

References

Godber, G. (1976). The confidential inquiry into maternal death. A limited study of clinical results. In *A Question of Quality: Roads to Assurance in Medical Care*, edited by G. McLachlan. London: Oxford University Press.

McColl, I. (1976). Observations on the quality of surgical care. In *A Question of Quality: Roads to Assurance in Medical Care*, edited by G. McLachlan. London: Oxford University Press.

McColl, I., Fernow, L. C., Mackie, C. and Rendall, M. (1976). Communication as a method of medical audit. *The Lancet*, **i**, 1341–1344.

Thompson, R. E. (1976). *New England Journal of Medicine*, **295**, 842.

Whitehead, T. (1976). Surveying the importance of pathological laboratories. In *A Question of Quality: Roads to Assurance in Medical Care*, edited by G. McLachlan. London: Oxford University Press.

The Health Centre

The Health Centre, Thorne, Near Doncaster, England

It is with great pleasure that I accepted the society's invitation to address you on *The Health Centre.*

We are now nearing the end of the meeting, during which you have heard many excellent lectures. I am reminded of an old Yorkshire cricket story. Hirst and Rhodes in their early days came together for the last wicket on the last day of a Test Match against Australia in 1902 with 15 runs needed to win. One said to the other, "Come on lad we'll nudge 'em in singles", and they did so.

I propose to do similarly. This lecture will be informal—no visual aids will be used and the only references come under the category of 'unpublished work', 'personal communication', etc. I intend merely to give you a little homily on the activities within a health centre. I shall then relate to you three interesting case histories, which I hope will provide you with illustrations of differing varieties of social repair, with which I have recently been associated. They will be, as it were, the last three singles to be nudged!

I have worked in a health centre for three years, and I often remark that I was born thirty years too early. Practice in a health centre is entirely different from practice as it was conducted from our own premises. I have found both most satisfying and enjoyable, but this new concept is an amazing advance—indeed I may say it is an exciting venture, involving especially, the social field of medicine in those many aspects which affect the community as a whole. Now, thanks also to the astonishing progress in medicine itself, work in a health centre can, and should, make general practice much more effective and useful in many ways. Ten years ago much general practice was conducted by the doctor in comparative isolation, often in competition, with little ancillary or para-medical aid, and often with insufficient space in which to operate. Now the scope of the work has expanded in many different directions.

Everything has to be defined of course these days, and so we must define a health centre. A patient somewhere has been quoted as saying: "A health centre is where I can collect my prescription, but it is difficult to get to see the doctor because of the receptionists."

Doctors are sometimes thought to be busy people who sign prescriptions, and who have to be protected from the 'phone as much as possible—presumably so that they can have more time for golf!

However, to be serious, I think of a health centre as a place where the doctor can meet, treat and discuss his patients. The word *discuss* is all important and involves colleagues and para-medical workers of all grades, and of varying qualifications.

The expression 'health centre' was first introduced about 1946, and replaced the word 'clinic' to describe the premises in which Local Health Authorities carried out public health work and preventive medicine. Gradually there emerged the idea of a centre to embrace many forms of medical care of the community including general practice.

Since 1948, the whole concept of health centres has been developed, and the number and variety of services is still expanding. Finance, organisation and coordination are key factors.

The cost of the service in its various forms is (as you have heard) very heavy. For example, our own health centre with six consulting suites, which was conceived ten years ago and completed three years ago cost £54,000. One at present being built in Doncaster, with three consulting suites, is scheduled to cost £118,000. Some enterprising practitioners have planned and built their own centres, but this is obviously a heavy burden.

I gather that the present government hope to accommodate about 15 per cent or so of general practitioners in centres by 1980. This seems to me to be a disappointingly low figure, and I think we are fortunate that in our industrial Doncaster area, with a population of roughly 280,000 people, there are nine centres for 62 doctors—with three more centres in the pipeline. If a general practitioner can cope with say 3000 patients, the outlay would be enormous to accommodate the whole population.

A centre consists briefly of a waiting area; a reception area with records etc., phones and offices; consulting and examination rooms; rooms for para-medical work; accommodation in which Health Authority work can proceed, and a common room for all staff—the latter an important room where much conversation consists of the exchange of medical information.

Now who are these strange creatures that inhabit these centres, and what do they do in the context of social repair?

I shall say little about doctors for, of necessity, they spend much time identifying and treating disease, though this, in itself, is bound up with social problems. They are, however, prime coordinators of much social work, that needs first, initiation and then completion.

Receptionists are key personnel and although much maligned at times and in some places, they learn a great deal about patients and their families, about their background, and often about their social problems. Their attitude and efficiency depends largely on their training within the practice, and this is all important. They are indeed subject to a lot of pressure, but they can be of immense help when social problems are being considered. All the other inhabitants of the building will be identified later, alongside the activities which take place within.

Now who uses the centre from outside? Well, the public of course, and that means all of us from time to time. I have, therefore, divided us into 14 groups in order to illustrate to you, as best I may, a few of the differing problems which may need social repair—and I am sure you will be able to think of many others. All groups are interrelated, and I have tried to avoid including purely medical matters.

First and Second

Babies, before and after birth—and tied up as it were with the umbilical cord—pregnant mothers:

Blood incompatibilities, congenital or birth abnormalities; multiple pregnancies. Abortion—accidental or otherwise. Stillbirth.
Mothers with wanted or unwanted children, by fathers, in name or only in person.

Three

Children up to school age:

One-parent families.
Step-parents. Orphans.
Adoption and fostering.

Four

Children up to leaving school:

School problems.
Illigitimacy.
Bullying of various sorts.
Enuresis.
Examinations.
IQ too low—and perhaps if we have present company in mind IQ very high—that is gifted children.

Five

Teenagers:

Broken homes.
Ill-chosen companions.
Delinquency. Adolescent sex.
Insecurity of youth.
Pregnancy. Too early marriage.
Parent problems.
Drugs and alcohol.

Six

Parents:

Housing.
Problems involved in rearing a family.
Marital.
School problems.
Step-children.
Infertility.
Birth control.

Seven

The male sex:

Employment.
The female sex.
Alcohol.

Eighth

The female sex:

The childless.
Too many children.
Financial stress.
The male sex and love affairs.
Outside jobs—part or full-time.
Menopausal.

Nine

Grandparents:

Living with their offspring and grandchil-
dren.
Lack of privacy.
Noise.
Responsibility for grandchildren and the
house, when parents are at work.

Ten

The elderly:

Isolation. Financial.
Reduced mobility. Infirmity.
Housing and accommodation.
Retirement.

Eleven

Widows and widowers:

Bereavement. Loneliness.
Insecurity.
Lack of interest and incentive.

Twelve

The disabled: Mental or physical disability.
                                       Dependency.
                                       Loss of mobility.
                                       Loneliness.
                                       Being different from others.
                                       Isolation. Sex problems.

Thirteen

Nearly last but by no means least: Housing.
divorcées or individuals living apart or   Financial.
cohabiting: Children.

Fourteen

Casualties and accidents: Pain and suffering.
                                       Mental shock.
                                       Change in circumstances.
                                       Law suits and compensation.
                                       Loss of job.

I will now list briefly the activities—sometimes called clinics—which can take place in a health centre. These are not necessarily complete, and they are increasing with time and experience:

Sessions for ante-natal and post-natal work; relaxation classes; family planning and cervical smears. The midwives attached to the practice by the Health Authority play an important part here. They visit the patient's home where necessary—in the ante-natal period and after discharge from hospital up to the tenth day (or longer if needed), or during the whole period if confinement takes place at home.

Immunisation; treatment of casualties; injections; dressings. These are carried out by Health Authority nurses attached to the practice, and often by a sister employed by the practice. The term 'District Nurse' used to be a beloved byword, but now they have all been upgraded to 'Home Sister'. I asked one of our pretty and attractive nurses the other day which term she preferred and she said charmingly, "Well, most people call me Lynn"!

Daily visits are carried out by these competent nurses, to patient's houses to carry out many forms of treatment and general nursing care, at all hours of the day, and sometimes at night, and this service is of prime importance in our context. Hospital services are thereby eased, and patients' travelling is reduced. The kindness and encouragement they give to patients and their families alike is of immense value. Their work is sometimes taken for granted nowadays, but they are key figures in social repair, and in daily contact with doctors, health visitors and social services.

Health visitors form a branch of the nursing profession that has really come into its own, in my view, in recent years. They are of great value in a health centre from a social repair angle, and they become even more valuable as their long and skilled training is realised and utilised by practitioners.

Health visitors used to be employed by Local Authorities on preventive aspects of family health, and they were concerned mainly with infant welfare clinics; assessment of children up to school age, and with school clinics. This work they still do, but when they are attached to general practitioners they are able to act as valuable catalysts between the family, the doctor and the social services, and so they are all important.

They can be asked to investigate all sorts of family difficulties. They can investigate, in the first place, such diverse matters as: children in care; children's school anxiety with its diverse symptomatology; enuresis; child neglect or cruelty; suspected baby battering; fractious or difficult babies and their effect on parents (and indeed on neighbours); school absenteeism or truantism; delinquency as it affects the home; advice to families regarding attendance, mobility or other allowances and aids, and many other problems too. All these jobs health visitors can undertake in conjunction with home sisters and with social services. I am not here discussing the latter most important service for it is a separate administration and is not, as a rule, incorporated in a health centre, though this has been envisaged and might well be useful. In any case, two way communication needs to be easy and effective between medical and social services.

Other services from health centres may include:

Chiropody

This is a free domiciliary and clinic service available to pensioners; the disabled; the blind and to diabetics.

Dental Care

This is provided by Health Authorities for schoolchildren and for pre- and post-natal mothers. It is a time and tooth-saving service for both children and parents.

Audiometry

A useful test for many, and in my view it can sometimes be especially important in children who are poor performers at school.

'Weight Watchers'

Usually done in group sessions supervised by health visitors. This is a popular class for weight reduction, which improves a woman's well-being, her morale and attractiveness, and so it can be an important repair process.

Men are usually blissfully unaware of these advantages as applied to themselves.

Dietician Clinic

A dietician attends to advise and supervise medically prescribed diets.

Geriatric Assessment

Elderly patients can be transported in vehicles, perhaps run by voluntary services, for assessment of their general health and well being.

Marriage Guidance Council

Such sessions held in the local health centre may be somewhat too near home to be entirely popular.

Physiotherapy; Occupational; Speech Therapy

All these most useful services are limited by finance and also by a shortage of skilled personnel. They are usually attractive young women, whose careers are often interrupted early, by marriage to medical men or to other perceptive individuals. Physiotherapy in particular could be a most important addition to general practice, and it could do much to hasten and help social repair. It is a service well worth development and support.

Psychiatric Nursing Service

This is a new and most helpful development. An experienced mental health nurse attends, to collate and assess information relating to a patient's psychiatric and social history, and formulates a planned, ongoing programme of care and supervision after consultation.

Hypertensive Clinic

This is to monitor hypertensives.

Dispensing

Drugs may be dispensed in country districts especially by the doctor or by a private chemist.

Consultants

They may visit and examine the patients, and this can accelerate diagnosis and treatment, and does save transport and the patient's time and effort.

Medical Students; Trainee Nurses and Doctors' Training for General Practice

These can all be attached from time to time to a centre, and so they are enabled to observe social problems in the field, at first hand.

Lectures and Meetings

These are of various groups and are held by arrangement.

A recent innovation has been a soiled dressings and clothing service to patient's homes, useful especially in smokeless zones, or where there is no fire in the house.

So there is really no limit to the type of help and special advice that can be given to all who are in contact with a health centre. Time, money, space and progressive planning are essential needs for doctors and Health Authorities alike.

I now have three stories to tell you; one of successful repair; one of failure, and the other 'I don't know', but you may be able to decide.

A short time ago I received a pathetic, four-page letter from an anxious lady in Blackpool, imploring me to help her partially blind and diabetic brother, aged 75, who is a patient of ours.

Briefly she said: "Oh! Doctor please get John into a home. My sister from Doncaster goes over and she says he is filthy, he doesn't stick to his diet and he eats everything. My mam spoiled him from being born and he has been a handful all his life, and naughty too. We are not posh, but by heaven we are clean. Please doctor tell him you want his flat for a family."

I asked our health visitor and our home sister to remind me of what we had already done, and to see what further help we could give. They told me that John had been housed in a council flat, that he walked daily to and from our old people's home where he stayed from 10 a.m. to 5 p.m. 5 days' weekly—transport provided if necessary—all meals provided; his washing was done and suits cleaned; outings on occasion with the other residents. All this cost him 35p per day. He has a home help, and has several times refused a permanent place in the home—and he still does. He manages his weekends in his own flat alright, and he is perfectly happy with his independence. I asked for weekends at the home for him subject to availability, and I wrote to Blackpool accordingly. I received a nice reply expressing thanks and adding, "God bless the people at the home".

This is not perfect repair perhaps, but it is, at any rate, reasonably successful.

Secondly, a very brief account of a case of baby battering:

The case consisted of an immature couple, married young, the husband at 16 and the wife at 19. He was illegitimate, brought up by grandparents with a poor background. He was a miner and did not work regularly. She was an aggressive girl with a formidable temper.

They had three children in quick succession. Two were cared for fairly well, but the middle one, John, was not. He had been a premature baby, a weakling; a small miserable child—always crying— probably because he was kept short of food. He was in hospital at four months old, with injuries sustained when mother was said to have fallen with him in her arms.

Suspicions were aroused, and our most conscientious and kindly health visitor visited the house every week for 15 months (believe it or not) and she developed a friendly liaison with the mother whom she thought was badly irritated by the husband's behaviour. John did not thrive, but no actual evidence of ill treatment to any of the children was ever discovered.

We had a consultant domiciliary visit, and the child was in hospital for one month for investigation, with negative results.

John had reached the age of 20 months, when a call was received from the husband to visit the baby. One of our more experienced receptionists took the call, and instinctively sensed that it was an urgent matter. I rushed along at once, and had to wait several minutes for the door to be unlocked for me. Normally in Thorne the doctor knocks and walks straight in.

I found the child John neatly dressed in clean tidy clothes lying in the middle of the living-room floor and obviously dead. Not a word was said while I examined the baby. I found to my horror 60 bruises and other marks on the body (a ruptured bowel was found at the post mortem). The three of us stood round looking at each other for fully half a minute in silence and we all knew why. Then a bizarre story was told, plainly fabricated in parts.

Thus John had been battered to death at 20 months by his mother. She was remanded at Risley and after conviction was sent for treatment to a prison hospital, and was released after only two months. The remaining two children were put into the care of her own mother until they are 18.

She and her husband are reunited, and are living in a private flat as opposed to a colliery house and all seems to be well.

And so, in spite of all, we have sadly failed in our efforts for this family—so far!

And now a brighter note with which to conclude:

Mr A. aged 62 has been a pleasant patient of mine for many years. He has a 'polio' arm and leg—the latter much shorter than the other, and so he has a pronounced limp. In addition, he exhibits violent shaking movements of the affected arm and leg, especially marked when anxious, or when talking to people. However, he gets about very well, particularly so on his pushbike, and then he invariably has a cigarette in his mouth which he does not remove.

Unfortunately, his wife suffered from multiple sclerosis, but nevertheless Mr 'A' had always held down a regular job and had worked well as a council gardener until his wife died. I then helped him to retire early on a pension.

Shortly after this, I received a request from the social services to approve of a telephone being installed for him, installation charges and rent to be paid for by them. This was in case he fell down in his second-floor flat and needed to send for his relatives, who live not far away. Mr 'A' had become a regular churchgoer and the vicar also asked if I could help to get a telephone installed. Our very attentive and conscientious MP very strongly supported the idea too.

My health visitor and I considered the matter in detail, and for some time I refused the request as I felt that the circumstances did not really justify the public expense.

However, so much pressure was applied to me, that in the end we decided to approve the application, but asked if the instrument could be put on the floor with extensions to each room so that if Mr 'A' fell down he could reach the phone. We did recommend primarily a ground-floor flat as being more useful, but this suggestion was not approved.

Very soon the instrument was installed on a high dresser. It is irrelevant to note that the phone is seldom used; that Mr 'A' has not been to church of late; and that the vicar has moved to Somerset!

Well, Ladies and Gentlemen, you may judge whether social repair was effected or not, but the last time I saw Mr 'A' on his cycle with his cigarette *in situ*, he gave me a friendly smile, touched his cap and gave me a wave of his 'polio' arm.

Acknowledgements

For information used in the preparation of this paper it is a pleasure to record thanks to: Mr R. Hill, Administrator, Health Centres and Clinics, Doncaster Area Health Authority; Mrs A. D. Jones, Senior Health Visitor, Thorne Health Centre, and her colleagues; and also to Mrs Joan Brennan for her clerical assistance.

Author Index

Numbers in italic indicate the page on which the full reference is given

Subject Index